The POTATO EXPERIENCE

The POTATO EXPERIENCE

Wonderful Ways with Potato Outers and Innards

RECIPES, ILLUSTRATIONS, CALLIGRAPHY
and HAND-LETTERING

by

Lisa Tanner

TEN SPEED PRESS
Berkeley, California

TEN SPEED PRESS
P.O. Box 7123
Berkeley, California 94707

Library of Congress Catalog Number:
ISBN: 0-89815-159-7

Cover illustration by Lisa Tanner

Library of Congress Cataloging-in-Publication Data

Tanner, Lisa.
    Potato Experience.

    Includes index.
    1. Cookery (Potatoes)   I. Title.
TX803.P8T36   1986   641.6'521   85–27922
ISBN 0–89815–159–7

Printed in the United States of America
10 9 8 7 6 5 4

This book is dedicated to you, Marian Edith Wolfson, for being such a wonderful, giving and loving mother. Thank you for all you have given us throughout the years. I love you very much.

ACKNOWLEDGMENTS:

I have some very special friends and family, and they deserve a few words of praise. Sincere thanks to...

Roberta, for being my very own one-of-a-kind sister.

Jessie, for letting me experience the joys (and frustrations) of motherhood, and especially for giving me so much love.

Paul, for being so supportive and accepting.

Lisa Jean and Mike, for your continual support and love in our everlasting friendship.

Robyn, for being such a good, honest and loyal friend.

Cheryl, for keeping me in the best of company during our many hours of jogging.

Lynn, for making the long journey on Highway 5 acquire a brand new meaning.

Mary, for being the unique and treasured friend you are.

Anna, for the wonderful memories we have shared, and for all that we have been through together.

Bill, for growing into the man I always knew you would be, and for helping me grow, too.

Debbie, for giving me the opportunity to get to know such a special, talented person — you.

Dennis, for entering my life and touching my heart so deeply.

...and lastly, my father Leonard, for giving me a lifetime of inner strength and for teaching me more than you will ever know.

Thank you.

The potato. Simplicity in its truest form. We Americans seem to adore them. We eat them mashed, fried and baked; diced, sliced and grated; hot or cold; plain or fancy. In fact, according to statistics, the average American consumes well over 100 pounds of potatoes per year!

What's behind this great love affair? Well, potatoes are versatile and economical. They're a natural, health-promoting vegetable and contain an abundance of vitamins and minerals (especially potassium), with only a trace of fat. But best of all, potatoes are just plain delicious.

Most of us, though—even the most dedicated potato lovers—have yet to discover the pleasures of eating the potato skin. We all enjoy that baked potato experience—mashing up the insides, loading them up with butter and gobs of sour cream, maybe adding a flourish of chives, and gobbling up the result. Maybe it's just a bad habit, but the majority of us will leave that edible shell, the skin, behind—meal after meal. The time has come to introduce you to the culinary possibilities of the humble potato skin and expose you to its true merits once and for all.

Potato skins lend themselves to almost any filling from all ethnic groups (how about a Taco Salad Skin or Egg Skins Florentine?). In this cookbook you will find recipes for everything from appetizers to full meals, from quiches to casseroles. There are special sections with vegetarian and low calorie recipes, and one devoted entirely to children. One section deals solely with "innards" because once you start eating potato skins, you may find yourself with an excess of leftover cooked potatoes! There is even a fantasy of sweet potato and yam recipes you won't want to miss. It's all here, waiting for you!

Lisa Tanner

November 1985

Table of Contents

continued...

Potato Basics

Unless otherwise specified, all of the potato skin rec~ipes are made with genuine "Russet" or "Idaho" potatoes; also known as "baking potatoes." Their skins are thick and flavorful, and become even tastier when "crisped" or "fried" to hold one of the many fillings you are about to encoun~ter.

The following information will help you make your choice when selecting potatoes to bake, scoop and stuff. In most supermarkets you'll find unbeatable prices on 5 and 10~pound bags of prepackaged potatoes. But look carefully through the wrapper. Sometimes the potatoes are green, shriveled and almost miniscule in size. That's no bargain!

Look for heavy, full~size potatoes (skinny is out). The surfaces should be smooth and firm without any soft spots. Green skins, as previously stated, are a no~no. What if they're sprouting? That's okay, as long as the potato is still firm and fresh looking. Just remove its sprouts.

MINI...MEDIUM...LARGE

about 3 to a pound

Mini potatoes make perfect skins for children because their size is not overwhelming to a small eater, and they can usually be picked up and eat~en without too much difficulty. They're great for lunch boxes, ready~made snacks, and don't forget about picnics, too. Mini skins make excel~lent party appetizers, miniature quiches, bite~size pizzas, etc. — anytime a finger food is de~sired.

about 2 to a pound

Medium potatoes are your average run~of~the~mill~size potatoes. When a potato this size is baked, halved, scooped, crisped and filled, two halves should satisfy a moderately hungry per~

11

son if the skins are accompanied by a salad or side dish of some sort. (That's two skins or one whole potato per person. Get it?) Confession: I have been known to consume a lot more than two skins at any one meal. Make adjustments according to how heavy your fillings are and to what extras you will be serving with the skins. Are the skins piled high with toppings like sour cream or cheese? Are they stuffed with meat or beans which are more filling than say, sautéed veggies? Are you planning lots of extras with your meal like salad, bread and a rich dessert? If so, the skins will go further.

about 1 pound each

Large potato skins are a meal! One per person is usually sufficient, and any more than two would certainly be pushing comfortableness. I prefer to use large skins because they hold much more filling and there's plenty of room for extravagant garnishing.

One last thought: If a recipe calls for six large potato skins, it will serve anywhere from three to six delighted people. If you have medium~size potatoes on hand, you can probably fill about eight or nine skins from that particular recipe —more with mini~size skins. This of course, is approximate, and depends on each individual recipe and how it's prepared. You'll soon get the hang of it.

Some Exceedingly Important Potato Definitions

1~ <u>Stuffed Potato Skin</u>: A baked potato, halved, scooped of its innards, crisped or fried, then filled with anything from melted cheese and fresh vegetables to eggs, beans, or spiced up chicken.

2~ <u>Stuffed Baked Potato</u>: A baked potato split open, hollowed of its innards, then filled with a tasty stuffing of potato innards combined with megadoses of sour cream, sautéed veggies, bacon, seasonings, etc., and rebaked until hot and crusty.

3~ <u>Topped Baked Potato</u>: A baked potato split open, and generously smothered by a robust soup or stew, buttery vegetables, creamy sauces, chunky gravies, etc., or even those seldom appreciated leftovers.

4~ <u>Potato Innards</u>: The "meat" of the potato, the scooped out insides that, when creatively treated, can be transformed into hearty dumplings, crispy croquettes, savory kugels, and other mouth-watering dishes.

The Art of Potato Skin Making

It takes just three easy steps to transform a friendly potato into a crispy, crunchy skin ready to be filled. First, the potato needs to be baked, then scooped of its innards, and finally either "crisped" or "fried" to perfection. Follow these simple directions, and you'll soon master the art of making potato skins.

Step #1. Preheat oven to 400°. Scrub the potatoes well under cold water and blot dry. You may wish to rub the entire skin with sweet or salted butter for more flavor and a moister texture. Prick each potato once or twice with a table knife. To prevent making holes where fillings may leak out later, prick the potatoes where you plan to cut them after baking. Baking time may be anywhere from 45 minutes for "mini's" to 1½ hours for the large variety. Potatoes are thoroughly baked if they feel soft when gently squeezed with a pot holder. Here's a valuable tip: When the potatoes are done, turn the oven off and let them sit uninterrupted until the oven cools down. This will toughen up the skins and give them that "potatoey" flavor you may have experienced when dining out. Don't leave them sitting for hours, though, or you will wind up with potato rocks.

Step #2. When the potatoes are cool, slice them lengthwise through the center with a sharp (preferably serrated) knife.* With a pointed spoon, scoop out the innards, leaving a small layer of potato coating the skin. If you scoop away all of the insides, the skin is likely to tear. This is espe~ cially important to remember when using a runny filling like quiche, for instance. Note: Don't you dare toss out those innards! See the chapter Wonderful Ways with Potato Innards.

*If the potatoes are small, you can just slide off a "lid" instead of cutting them entirely in half. This will give you extra space for the filling. In this case, one potato equals one skin or "shell."

14

⬭ = 2 skins   ⬭ = 1 skin or "shell"

Step #3. To Crisp or to Fry ??? It's purely a matter of taste...

Crisped Skins: Place the scooped out skins on a baking sheet or tray, brush them with enough melted butter to coat their surfaces nicely, then sprinkle lightly with salt or seasoned salt. (The salt is optional.) Bake at 400° for about 10 minutes, or broil at close watch until they are as crispy as you like. If you enjoy extra crunchy skins, broil them until they start to sizzle and brown. If a recipe calls for "lightly crisped" skins, bake or broil the skins only until they are hot and the edges just start to crispen. If the recipe calls for skins that are hot, use them straight out of the oven or reheat for a brief period of time, covering them with foil if you want them to stay moist.

Fried Skins: To do a good job of frying potato skins, you need enough oil (2 to 3 inches deep) to submerge the skins totally. Keep the oil at a constant temperature of 375°. A deep fat fryer or a frying thermometer will take out the guesswork. Gently lower the skins into the hot oil and fry for 2 or 3 minutes, or until they turn golden brown inside and crispy outside. Supervise closely. Remove them carefully with a slotted spoon or spatula and drain face-side down on paper towels. This is the time to salt the skins if you like. Note: It is important to leave that extra layer of potato when scooping out the innards so the fried skins don't burn or get too brittle.

Preparing Potato Shells for Quiche Fillings

Any size potato skin makes a perfect "crust" for your favorite quiche recipe. Use mini potato skins for appetizer quiches, and large ones when serving them as a main course. Kids especially love quiches baked in a crusty potato shell—they're the ultimate in finger food.

Since quiches are essentially a rich and savory custard, they need precious oven time to solidify properly. This is why in all of the following quiche recipes, I call for potato skins which are "lightly crisped." They'll get crispier as they bake in the oven.

This brings us to the most important point: Since quiche fillings start out as a liquid (before baking), the prepared shells must be free from holes and cracks so they won't leak. To insure this, leave a slightly thicker layer of potato when scooping out the skins before "crisping" them. Handle the potato shells carefully too, for they can become quite temperamental.

One last word of advice: Use potato skins that have a nice rim to them. They'll hold more filling and are less likely to overflow. Fill the potato shells not quite to the top so they can be easily transferred to the oven.

Make Ahead Skins

Next time you bake a batch of potatoes to scoop and stuff, bake up a whole bunch and freeze the extra scooped out skins. Stack them carefully for storage, and wrap them in airtight plastic bags or put them in plastic freezer containers for adequate protection. The skins may become a bit icy in your freezer depending on how long they are stored and how tightly they're wrapped, but should be just fine after they're cooked. Simply thaw them (at room temperature or in a microwave oven) and crisp or fry them as usual. Unfilled skins are convenient for making the most of last night's leftovers or for composing tasty appetizers and snacks in record time.

As for refrigerating and freezing already stuffed skins, there are a few points to keep in mind. Almost all the recipes in this book can be frozen quite successfully, but it is best to avoid ones that contain raw vegetables with a high water content (tomatoes, for instance) or the delicate soufflé type skins. They will taste much better freshly made.

Some cheesy fillings freeze better than others. The same goes for egg, sauce, or meat mixtures. So experiment with your favorite recipes. Freeze, thaw, heat and taste, then decide for yourself.

Wrap filled skins extra tight in plastic bags (foil or freezer containers work, too) and seal them well. You may wish to lay them on a cookie sheet first and freeze them until they are almost solid. The skins will then stack up very nicely for storage, and there will be less chance of damage. You can thaw them before heating, or heat them still frozen, covered with foil, in a moderate oven until completely hot. Hold off on sensitive garnishes like sour cream until just before serving.

Note: If the recipe calls for baking the skins for an ex-

17

tended period of time (as in a quiche), be sure this is done _prior_ to refrigerating or freezing.

Using Seasoned Salt

In this book, you'll find many recipes calling for seasoned salt rather than plain table salt. This is because I discovered that the seasoned variety sometimes brings out more flavor in a recipe and perhaps adds that extra "zing" it may be missing. You can, of course, substitute regular table salt if you prefer.

There are lots of tasty seasoning salts on the market today. Most contain a higher dosage of salt than anything else, usually followed by a multitude of dehydrated vegetables, herbs, and possibly some sugar and unmentionable additives. Natural food stores sell seasoned or "herb" salts that contain no sugar or preservatives in case you choose to avoid such things. There are also seasoning blends that are low in sodium if you are restricting your intake of salt. Try out a few brands until you find your very favorite.

Wonderful

POTATO RECIPES

Appetizers, Munchies and Noshes

Sometimes you're in the mood for "just a little something." It may be before a meal, between meals, or even at some ungodly hour (1:00 a.m. for example). Or maybe you need some crowd~pleasing snacks for a party or picnic. Believe me, the most fulfilling answer to your prayers can be found in one word~ POTATO (of course).

Picture a sizzling array of mini~size po~ tato skins dripping with melted cheese at your next informal gathering. Imagine a buffet table with an extraordinary selection of dips surrounded by crispy Skin Chips. Think of how utterly wonderful it would be to sink your teeth into a hot stuffed potato skin next time you arrive home late, tired and famished.

In this chapter you'll find some great solutions to your munchie problems. You will be introduced to Skin Chips, to a myriad of unique dips and spreads, and to other sim~ ple and fun recipes that will make quick nib~ bling more enjoyable than ever before.

The Marvels of Skin Chips

Potato chips have been around for decades. This crispy, salty, somewhat greasy snack food is a favorite lunch box treat with children as well as a welcome party food for grown-ups. One of their main attributes is the way they scoop up dips and spreads. They are also quite irresistible once you sample just a few.

But, alas, potato chips have been labeled as one of the most infamous "junk foods" of our time. Basically, they're thought to contain more oil and salt than potato, and many of the chips on the market today are flavored with artificial cheese and other not-so-healthy man-made additions. Even the so-called "natural" chips aren't all that much better.

This brings me to the introduction of Skin Chips — pleasingly crunchy, perfectly seasoned chips you make yourself from baked potato skins. They're wonderful for scooping up dips, for simple noshing, to accompany soups and sandwiches, or for dunking into that old standby — catsup. You can control the size and shape, and the amount of oil, salt and seasonings to your exact specifications. Ingenious, huh?

Skin Chips are made almost exactly like a potato skin you would "crisp" or "fry" for a main dish (see page 15). Begin with a baked potato; cut it in half and scoop out the insides. (Note: The more potato you leave attached to the skin, the more flavorful and "potatoey" your skin chips will be.) Cut the skins into desired sizes. Larger chips are best for scooping up dips, while smaller ones can be munched upon with a sandwich or sprinkled on hot soups for extra crunch.

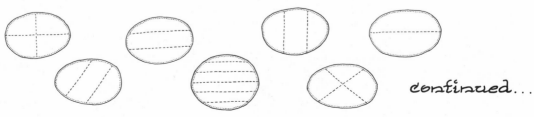

continued...

To _crisp_: Brush the pieces with enough melted butter to coat their surfaces nicely. Broil (baking may not get them crispy enough) and season to your liking.

To _fry_: Heat 2 or 3 inches of oil to 375°. Fry skin chips 30 seconds to 1 minute, depending on the size and on how crispy and crunchy you like them. Remove from oil and drain well on paper towels. Season to your liking.

BROILING VS FRYING

Broiling ～

Pro: More convenient than deep frying.

Pro: Less fattening because you only brush the skins with butter instead of submerging them in oil.

Con: Not as crispy or tasty.

Frying ～

Pro: Makes crispier, crunchier chips with the wonderful toasty flavor of deep fried potatoes.

Con: More fattening.

Con: More time consuming to make.

SKIN CHIP SEASONING GUIDE

～ grated Parmesan or Romano cheese
～ barbecue seasoning
～ garlic and/or onion salt
～ favorite dried herbs
～ soy sauce or teriyaki sauce
～ seasoned salt or pepper
～ Mexican seasoning

Chunky Guacamole Dip

2 large ripe avocados
1 tablespoon lemon juice
2 tablespoons sour cream
2 cloves garlic, crushed
⅓ cup diced green chili peppers
1 small onion, finely chopped
1 medium-size tomato, diced and drained
1 hard-cooked egg, chopped (optional)
¼ to ½ teaspoon salt
Fresh black pepper <u>and</u> Tabasco to taste

Garnishes {
  shredded cheddar and/or Jack cheese
  chopped olives
  crumbled cooked bacon
  chopped scallions
  whole peppers
  parsley sprigs
  sour cream
  chopped tomatoes
}

In a medium-size bowl, mash avocados (leaving a few chunks). Add the lemon juice and all remaining ingredients except the garnishes. Chill well.

Spread the guacamole in a large flat bowl, making a smooth even surface. Decorate with circles of garnishes laid pinwheel-fashion on top. Serve with a basket of freshly cooked Skin Chips for scooping.

Makes about 2 cups.

23

Spicy Pinto Dip

Fabulous flavor.

1 cup raw pinto beans
3 slices bacon, diced
½ cup <u>each</u> minced onion and green bell pepper
2 cloves garlic, crushed
¾ teaspoon salt
½ teaspoon chili powder
¼ teaspoon cumin
Fresh black pepper
½ cup packed grated cheddar cheese
2 tablespoons sour cream

Garnish {crumbled cooked bacon

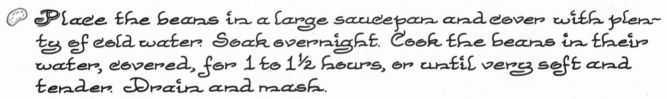

Place the beans in a large saucepan and cover with plenty of cold water. Soak overnight. Cook the beans in their water, covered, for 1 to 1½ hours, or until very soft and tender. Drain and mash.

In a large skillet, fry bacon until crisp. Drain and crumble, reserving drippings. In hot drippings, sauté onion, green pepper and garlic until soft. Add the mashed beans, salt, chili powder, cumin and black pepper, mixing well.

Over low heat, blend in the cheddar cheese until melted, then the sour cream and half the bacon.

Spoon bean mixture into a serving bowl and sprinkle with the remaining bacon. Serve warm or chilled, with plenty of Skin Chips.

Makes 2 generous cups.

Seven Layer Fiesta Dip

A munchers paradise.

1 16-oz. can refried beans, or 1 recipe Spicy Pinto Dip
  (page 24)
1 cup packed grated cheddar cheese
1 cup guacamole (see Chunky Guacamole Dip, page 23)
½ cup sour cream
½ cup chopped olives
1 medium-size tomato, chopped and drained
1 or 2 scallions, thinly sliced

Garnish {fresh cilantro or parsley sprigs

◎ Heat the beans gently in a saucepan until hot and
steamy. Pour them onto a large round dinner plate or
platter and spread with a spatula or spoon to make an
even layer. Sprinkle on the cheese to melt. (You can
stick this in an oven or microwave to hasten the melting
process.)

◎ Gently spread on the guacamole, leaving a little rim of
the beans and cheese to show. Follow the same way
with the sour cream, olives and tomatoes. (The layers
will resemble a dart board pattern. Be sure to make layers, not just circles of condiments.)

◎ Finish with a nice pile of scallions in the "bull's-eye"
position. Garnish the dip with cilantro sprigs and serve
right away—while the beans and cheese are warm.
<u>P.S.</u> Don't forget about the basket of warm Skin Chips.
That's the best part!

Makes about 5 cups.

sour cream   beans

guacamole

melted cheddar

Bleu Cheese & Toasted Almond Dip

2 3-oz. packages cream cheese, softened
¼ cup sour cream
¼ cup crumbled bleu cheese (1 oz.)
½ teaspoon Worcestershire sauce

¼ cup finely chopped toasted blanched almonds
2 tablespoons chopped black olives
1 tablespoon finely minced onion
Pinch of freshly minced garlic (optional)

Garnishes {
thinly sliced radishes
more olives
more almonds
apple wedges (dipped in lemon juice)
parsley sprigs

In a medium-size bowl, beat cream cheese with sour cream until very smooth and creamy. Thoroughly blend in the bleu cheese and Worcestershire.

Add all remaining ingredients except the garnishes. Cover and chill. Garnish as desired with any of the above suggestions. Serve with warm Skin Chips and fresh vegetable sticks.

Makes about 1⅓ cups.

Note: Chilled dip may need to be thinned with a little milk to achieve the proper consistency for scooping.

Cheddar & Bacon Dip

All your favorites — in one dip!

1½ cups sour cream
1 cup packed finely grated cheddar cheese
¼ cup each minced onion and green bell pepper
2 tablespoons diced pimento
1 clove garlic, finely minced
¼ teaspoon seasoned salt
Tabasco to taste
8 slices bacon, crisply cooked and finely crumbled

- In a medium-size bowl, mix sour cream with remaining ingredients (reserving a tablespoon or 2 of bacon for the garnish).

- Pile the dip into a serving bowl and sprinkle the top with the reserved bacon. Cover and chill well.

- Serve with warm Skin Chips and assorted raw vegetable dippers.

Makes 2 cups.

Note: If the dip becomes too thick, thin with a little milk.

Mini Quiche Skins

20 mini potato skins, lightly crisped

1 tablespoon butter
½ cup chopped mushrooms
⅓ cup diced onion
1 small clove garlic, finely minced
½ cup diced Italian salami
1⅓ cups finely grated Swiss cheese

4 eggs
1⅓ cups sour cream
2 tablespoons chopped parsley
1 teaspoon salt
Fresh black pepper

Topping & Garnish
{ grated Parmesan cheese
{ 10 cherry tomatoes, sliced
{ 20 olive slices or halves

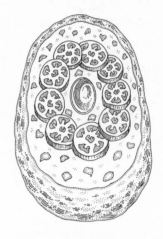

◎ Preheat oven to 375°. Melt butter in a small skillet and sauté mushrooms, onion and garlic until tender. Stir in salami, then remove from heat and cool. Mix in the Swiss cheese.

◎ In a bowl, beat eggs well. Thoroughly blend in sour cream, parsley, salt and pepper.

◎ Place an equal amount of the salami~Swiss cheese mix~ ture into each skin. Carefully spoon on the beaten cus~ tard, filling to the tops. Sprinkle skins with Parmesan.

◎ Bake about 20 minutes, or until just set but not brown. Remove skins from oven and top with tomato slices and olives. Sprinkle with more Parmesan. Bake 5 minutes longer, or until puffy and lightly golden brown.

Makes 20 mini skins.

Lox & Cream Cheese Skins

The perfect nosh.

6 to 8 mini potato skins, crisped or fried and hot
2 3-oz. packages cream cheese, softened
About 2 oz. lox, cut into 6 to 8 pieces

Garnishes
- minced scallions or chives
- parsley sprigs
- sliced or chopped olives
- seasonings (salt, pepper, paprika, dill weed, etc.)
- finely chopped mushrooms
- seeded and chopped tomatoes
- seeded and chopped cucumber
- sliced or chopped hard-cooked eggs

🥔 With an electric mixer, beat cream cheese until fluffy. Spread some cream cheese over each hot skin, and top with a thin slice of lox.

🥔 Garnish with any of the above suggestions, or serve the garnishes separately so each nosher is free to create a personal masterpiece.

Makes 6 to 8 mini skins.

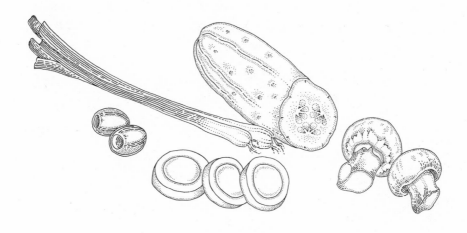

Creamy Smoked Fish Skins

16 mini potato skins, crisped or fried

2 3-oz. packages cream cheese, softened
¼ cup mayonnaise
¼ cup chopped black olives
2 scallions, minced
2 teaspoons finely diced pimento
7 to 8 oz. smoked fish, boned and flaked *

Garnish {parsley sprigs

 In a mixing bowl, blend cream cheese and mayon-naise until smooth. Stir in remaining ingredients except garnish, blending well.

Spread a generous amount of filling into each skin. Broil until hot and bubbly.

Serve the skins on a large platter, each garnished with a parsley sprig.

Makes 16 mini skins.

*Salmon, halibut, swordfish, etc.

Ultimate Nacho Skins

You'll be famous for these!

16 mini potato skins, crisped or fried

2 cups grated cheddar or Jack cheese, firmly packed
Sliced or diced canned green chili peppers (seeded)

◊ Preheat oven to 400°. Place skins on a baking tray. Sprinkle 2 tablespoons cheese evenly over each skin and top with a chili pepper strip or a few diced chilies.

◊ Bake about 10 minutes, or until cheese is melted and hot. Serve right away.

Makes 16 mini skins.

For Ultimate Bean & Cheese Nacho Skins:

~ Spread each skin with 2 tablespoons refried beans (canned or homemade), then sprinkle on the cheese and chilies and bake as directed above. You'll need 1 15-oz. can or 2 cups refried beans to complete 16 mini skins.

Nacho Toppings & Garnishes:

~ Add these toppings prior to baking...

* sliced black olives
* sautéed mushrooms
* chunks of spicy chicken or beef tucked under the melting cheese

~ Add these garnishes just before serving...

* salsa
* sour cream
* sliced scallions
* chunks of avocado

* diced tomatoes
* guacamole
* fresh cilantro sprigs

Curried Tuna & Egg Skins

Rich and wonderful, with a mild curry flavor.

14 mini potato skins, crisped or fried

2 3-oz. packages cream cheese, softened

¼ cup mayonnaise

1 6½-oz. can tuna, drained and flaked

2 hard-cooked eggs, finely chopped

¼ cup each minced scallions, chopped olives, and chopped
   toasted almonds

1 tablespoon diced pimento

1 teaspoon lemon juice

½ teaspoon curry powder

¼ teaspoon salt

Fresh black pepper

Topping { ½ cup sliced raw almonds
          grated Parmesan, cheddar or Jack cheese

Garnish { 14 olive slices

In a mixing bowl, beat cream cheese with mayonnaise until smooth. Blend in remaining ingredients except topping and garnish.

Stuff skins with tuna mixture. Top each with some sliced almonds and grated cheese.

Broil until topping is golden brown and filling is hot. Garnish each skin with an olive slice.

Makes 14 mini skins.

Onion~Cheese Fondue Skins

16 mini potato skins, crisped or fried

2 tablespoons butter

1 large clove garlic, finely chopped

2 medium-size onions, thinly sliced

2 cups thinly sliced mushrooms

Salt and fresh black pepper to taste

1 teaspoon dry sherry

Topping
{
2 cups grated Jack cheese
1 cup croutons
grated Parmesan cheese
}

Preheat oven to 400°. Melt butter in a large skillet. Sauté garlic, onions and mushrooms until soft and tender. Season with salt and pepper, then blend in the sherry, mixing well.

Pile a healthy amount of the sautéed vegetables into each skin. Sprinkle each with Jack cheese, then with the croutons. Dust Parmesan generously over all.

Bake skins for about 10 minutes, or until cheese is thoroughly melted and croutons are golden brown. Serve them hot.

Makes 16 mini skins.

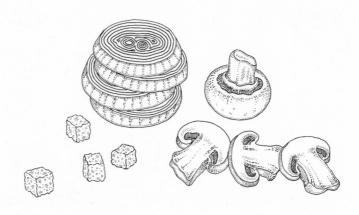

Dilled Shrimp Hors d'Oeuvre Skins

Everyone will adore these.

16 mini potato skins, crisped or fried

2 3-oz. packages cream cheese, softened
¼ cup mayonnaise
¼ cup finely chopped green bell pepper
1 tablespoon diced pimento
1 teaspoon lemon juice
¼ teaspoon each seasoned salt and dill weed
Tabasco to taste
8 oz. cooked shrimp, chopped

Topping { grated Parmesan cheese
{ paprika

Garnish { sliced black olives

- In a medium~size bowl, beat cream cheese with may~ onnaise until smooth. Blend in bell pepper, pimento, lemon juice, seasoned salt, dill weed, Tabasco and shrimp, mixing well.

- Fill each skin with the shrimp mixture. Sprinkle the tops with Parmesan, then dust with paprika.

- Broil until golden brown and puffy. Place an olive slice atop each hot skin and serve.

Makes 16 mini skins.

Cheese~Broiled Appetizer Skins

SHRIMP · ANCHOVIES · GUACAMOLE

10 mini potato skins, crisped or fried

1¼ to 1½ packed cups grated or sliced cheese ~ about 6 oz.
   (Try Jack, mild to sharp cheddar, Brie, mozzarella,
   all types of Swiss, etc.)

🦐 Place the skins on a baking tray. Sprinkle cheese (or lay slices) evenly into each skin.

✗ Broil until cheese melts and starts to bubble.

◍ Serve hot, by themselves, or topped with any of the following ideas:

   ~ crumbled cooked bacon or soy bacon bits
   ~ chopped tomatoes or cherry tomatoes
   ~ sliced black or pimento~stuffed olives
   ~ toasted nuts or seeds
   ~ chopped fresh veggies: cucumbers, mushrooms, radishes, zucchini...
   ~ favorite herbs
   ~ sliced scallions or chopped chives
   ~ diced ham or cooked Italian sausage or salami
   ~ whole shrimp or flaked crab meat
   ~ marinated artichoke hearts (cut up if large)
   ~ guacamole or diced avocado
   ~ sour cream
   ~ sliced jalapeños or diced green chilies
   ~ sautéed onion rings
   ~ sweet miniature pickles (whole or sliced)
   ~ anchovies

Makes 10 mini skins.

Note: Serve your hot cheesy skins with a bowl of cool sour cream for dipping and dunking.

Caviar Appetizer Skins

Desired number of potato skins, crisped or fried and _hot_

Favorite caviar (about 1 tablespoon per person)

Sour cream
Sieved hard~cooked egg yolks
Chopped hard~cooked egg whites
Diced onion
Lemon wedges
Snipped chives
Whipped cream cheese

- Place the caviar in a small clear dish set into a larger dish filled with crushed ice.

- Surround with a basket of hot skins along with separate bowls of the remaining accompaniments. Serve with chilled dry champagne.

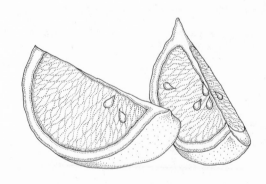

Clam Fondue Skins

Better than clam dip!

8 mini potato skins, crisped or fried

2 3-oz. packages cream cheese, softened
2 tablespoons dry white wine
1 small clove garlic, finely minced
1 scallion, finely minced
½ cup grated Parmesan cheese
¼ teaspoon Worcestershire sauce
Dash of Tabasco
1 6½-oz. can minced clams, drained

Topping { ¼ cup dry sourdough bread crumbs or crushed croutons

Optional Garnish { chopped parsley

- In a medium-size bowl, beat cream cheese until fluffy. Beat in the wine and garlic. Fold in scallion, Parmesan, Worcestershire, Tabasco and clams, mixing well.

- Pile the filling into each skin. Sprinkle each with some bread crumbs, and press them down slightly with your fingertips.

- Broil until filling is hot (watch closely!) and crumbs are nicely browned. Sprinkle with parsley if you like.

Makes 8 mini skins.

Salad and Sandwich Skins

This isn't a normal salad and sandwich chapter, but of course this isn't an everyday run-of-the-mill cookbook, either. To begin with, we feature sizzling <u>hot</u> salads, instead of the usual cold ones you are accustomed to eating. This is because all the salads are comfortably nestled upon hot crispy potato skins. Salad Skins can be the focal point of a meal, or can be served as a warming side dish for brunch, lunch or supper. Keep in mind that the potato skin or "shell" adds extra substance.

As for Sandwich Skins — it's really quite simple. Whatever you can pile on plain bread can be piled into a potato skin. And voilà!...The Sicilian Sausage Sub...a savory Monte Cristo... a Hot Cashew Chicken Melt...all improved via a hot and crispy potato shell. Sandwich Skins are served "open face" and hot. They can be taken along on picnics (in an insulated container), enjoyed at backyard gatherings, reheated at the office for a very distinguished lunch, or enjoyed any time an ordinary sandwich just doesn't tickle your fancy.

Crab, Avocado & Cashew Salad Skins

5 large potato skins, lightly crisped

6 oz. flaked cooked crab meat

⅓ cup each diced celery and chopped toasted cashews

1 small ripe avocado (peeled, pitted and cubed)

2 hard-cooked eggs, chopped

1 or 2 minced scallions

2 tablespoons diced pimento

⅓ cup mayonnaise

1 teaspoon lemon juice

½ teaspoon seasoned salt

Fresh black pepper

Topping
& Garnish { ¾ cup croutons — your favorite

🌸 Preheat oven to 400°. In a mixing bowl, lightly toss crab with remaining ingredients except croutons.

🌸 Fill skins with crab mixture. Bake 10 minutes, uncovered. Top each with its share of croutons, and continue baking 5 minutes longer, or until filling is hot and croutons are golden brown.

Makes 5 large skins.

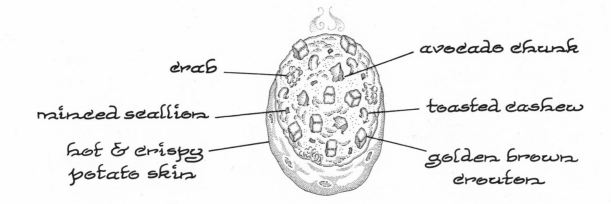

crab

avocado chunk

minced scallion

toasted cashew

hot & crispy potato skin

golden brown crouton

Curried Chicken Salad Skins

6 to 8 large potato skins, lightly crisped

3 cups chopped or slivered cooked chicken
1 cup diced tart apple
½ cup each diced celery and green bell pepper
½ cup chopped toasted peanuts or almonds
1 tablespoon grated onion

¾ cup mayonnaise
6 tablespoons sour cream
¾ teaspoon (more to taste) curry powder
Pinch sugar
Salt and pepper to taste

Garnish { romaine leaves
         { dark or golden raisins

🍃 Preheat oven to 350°. In a mixing bowl, lightly toss chicken with apple, celery, green pepper, peanuts and onion.

🍃 In a small bowl, mix mayonnaise with sour cream, curry, sugar, salt and pepper. Fold this gently into the chicken mixture.

🍃 Place the skins on a baking tray and stuff each with the chicken filling. Cover tightly with foil. Bake 20 to 30 minutes, or until heated through.

🍃 Arrange the hot baked skins on a bed of romaine. Garnish the tops with a sprinkling of raisins.

Makes 6 to 8 large skins.

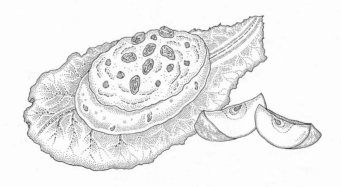

Hot German Potato Salad Skins

8 large potato skins, crisped or fried and hot

6 slices bacon
1 cup chopped onion
½ cup chopped green bell pepper
1 clove garlic, minced
2 tablespoons each flour and sugar
1½ to 2 teaspoons salt
1 teaspoon celery seed
Fresh black pepper
1 cup water
½ cup vinegar
½ cup thinly sliced radishes
3 lbs. potatoes, cooked and thinly sliced *

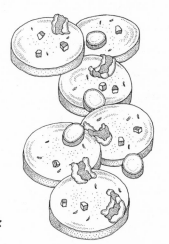

Garnish { 2 hard-cooked eggs, sliced
          paprika

- In a large skillet, fry bacon until crisp. Drain on paper towels, reserving drippings. Crumble bacon and set aside. In hot drippings, sauté onion, green pepper and garlic until onion is soft and pepper is bright green.

- Add the flour, sugar, salt, celery seed and black pepper. Cook until thick. Remove from heat and slowly blend in water and vinegar. Bring to a boil, stirring constantly. Simmer and stir 2 minutes longer, or until nicely thickened. Add the radishes, potatoes and crumbled bacon to the skillet. Heat gently, until all is uniformly hot.

- Fill the skins with potato mixture. Top each with an equal amount of sliced egg and dust lightly with paprika.

Makes 8 large skins.

*Or use about 6 cups of cooked potato innards.

Romanian Salad Skins

6 large potato skins, crisped or fried and hot

1 tablespoon olive oil

1 clove garlic, minced

1 medium~size onion, sliced

1 small green and 1 small red bell pepper, cut into strips

½ teaspoon each basil and red wine vinegar

¼ teaspoon salt

Fresh black pepper

1 medium~size tomato, coarsely chopped

½ cup each cooked garbanzo beans and diced Italian sala~
mi

¼ cup halved or sliced black olives

Garnish { grated Romano cheese
        { romaine leaves

Heat oil in a large skillet. Sauté garlic and onion until slightly tender. Add the green and red peppers, basil, vine~gar, salt and black pepper to taste. Stir for a minute, then cover and cook gently for approximately 10 minutes, or un~til vegetables are perfectly tender.

Uncover the skillet and stir in all remaining ingredients except the garnish. Continue to cook and stir 5 more min~utes, until all elements are heated through.

Pile the vegetable mixture into the awaiting hot skins. Sprinkle each with Romano cheese and serve on a bed of romaine leaves.

Makes 6 large skins.

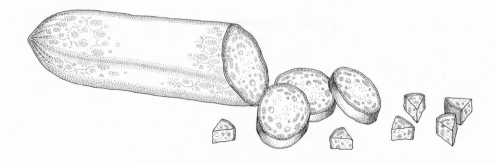

42

Hot & Tangy Bean Salad Skins

6 large potato skins, crisped or fried and hot

4 slices bacon
⅓ cup sugar
1 tablespoon cornstarch
¾ teaspoon salt
Fresh black pepper
6 tablespoons vinegar
¼ cup water

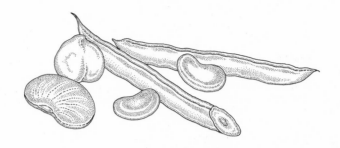

1 cup each cooked garbanzo beans, kidney beans, lima beans,
    and green beans
1 small red onion, thinly sliced
½ cup diagonally sliced celery

Garnish { 1½ cups finely shredded green cabbage
          crumbled bacon

Fry bacon in a medium~size skillet until crisp. Drain, reserving drippings. Crumble bacon and set aside. Into drippings, blend in sugar, cornstarch, salt and pepper. Stir in vinegar and water. Bring to a boil, stirring continuously until very thick.

Mix the beans into the hot skillet mixture. Simmer gently, uncovered, until very hot—about 15 minutes—stirring frequently. The last 5 minutes or so, blend in ½ of the crumbled bacon, the onion and celery.

Place equal amounts of cabbage in each skin. Generously spoon on the hot bean salad, and top with the remaining crumbled bacon.

Makes 6 large skins.

43

Hot Tuna Almond Salad Skins

A tantalizing blend of tuna, toasty nuts, and delicate sea~
sonings.

8 large potato skins, lightly crisped
2 6½~oz. cans solid white tuna, drained
1½ cups diced celery
1 cup croutons
⅔ cup chopped toasted almonds
2 hard~cooked eggs, chopped
2 scallions, thinly sliced on diagonal
2 tablespoons crumbled cooked bacon or soy bacon bits
1 cup mayonnaise
2 tablespoons lemon juice
½ teaspoon seasoned salt
Fresh black pepper
Dash or 2 of dill weed

Topping
&
Garnish
{ 1 cup croutons
¾ cup shredded Jack cheese, packed
paprika

- Preheat oven to 400°. In a large bowl, flake tuna. Com~
bine lightly with all the remaining ingredients except
topping and garnish.

- Stuff skins generously with tuna mixture. Top with 1 cup
croutons and sprinkle with the Jack cheese. Dust each
delicately with paprika.

- Bake uncovered about 15 minutes, or until thoroughly
hot and cheese is melted.

Makes 8 large skins.

Taco Salad Skins

6 to 7 large potato skins, crisped or fried and hot

1 lb. lean ground beef
1 onion, diced
1 small green bell pepper, chopped
1 clove garlic, crushed
1 8~oz. can tomato sauce
1 medium~size tomato, chopped
1½ teaspoons chili powder
¾ teaspoon salt
½ teaspoon honey or sugar
Fresh black pepper
Tabasco to taste
2 tablespoons sliced pimento~stuffed olives

Topping & Garnish
- 2 cups finely shredded lettuce, packed
- 1 cup grated cheddar cheese
- ½ cup lightly crushed corn chips
- 1 small tomato, diced
- 2 scallions, sliced

◉ In a medium~size skillet, sauté beef with onion, green pepper and garlic until meat loses its pink color. Drain off any fat. Add tomato sauce, chopped tomato, chili powder, salt, honey, black pepper and Tabasco. Cover the skillet and simmer very gently for 1 hour, stirring frequently, until thick and flavorful. Stir in olives the last 15 minutes or so.

◉ Fill each skin with an equal amount of lettuce, followed by a generous dosage of hot meat mixture. Top with cheese, then chips, diced tomato and scallions. Serve hot.

Makes 6 to 7 large skins.

Afterthought: A cup of cooked kidney beans may be added to the simmering meat mixture along with the olives. This will stretch the recipe to yield 8 or 9 skins.

Baked Salmon & Egg Salad Skins

6 or 7 large potato skins, lightly crisped

2 7½~oz. cans pink salmon

4 or 5 hard~cooked eggs, chopped

⅔ cup diced celery

½ cup each steamed green peas and chopped water chest~
   nuts

¼ cup each minced onion, sliced black olives and diced pimento

2 tablespoons lemon juice

⅔ cup mayonnaise

1 teaspoon salt

Fresh black pepper

Pinch of dill weed

Cayenne to taste

~⅔ cup shredded cheddar cheese~

Topping {
   ¼ cup dry bread crumbs
   2 tablespoons grated Parmesan cheese
   2 teaspoons melted butter

Garnish {chopped parsley

Preheat oven to 400°. Drain salmon and remove any bones and skin. Flake into a large bowl. Blend in all remaining ingredients except the cheddar cheese, topping and garnish.

Pile an adequate amount of salmon salad into each skin. Top with cheddar. In a small bowl, mix all topping ingre~ dients and sprinkle over the skins.

Bake uncovered 15 to 20 minutes, or until filling is hot and crumbs are nicely browned. Garnish with parsley.

Makes 6 to 7 large skins.

For extra crunch and zip, how about adding some chopped toasted almonds and a dash of soy sauce?

Wilted Cabbage, Potato & Apple Salad Skins

8 large potato skins, crisped or fried and hot

8 slices bacon
½ cup chopped onion
1 clove garlic, crushed
¼ cup each vinegar and water
2 tablespoons sugar
1 teaspoon salt
Fresh black pepper
Pinch caraway seed

6 to 8 cups shredded green cabbage
2 cups diced cooked potatoes
2 cups chopped red apples (unpeeled)

Garnish { crumbled bacon

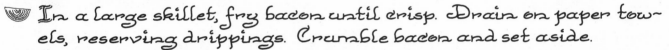

- In a large skillet, fry bacon until crisp. Drain on paper towels, reserving drippings. Crumble bacon and set aside.

- In ⅓ cup drippings, sauté onion and garlic until soft. Blend in vinegar, water, sugar and seasonings. Bring mixture to a boil, then stir in cabbage, potatoes and apples. Cover and cook over medium heat until cabbage is just wilted, about 3 to 5 minutes.

- Pile the cabbage mixture generously into each skin. Sprinkle the tops with crumbled bacon and serve hot.

Makes 8 large skins.

Ham, Cheddar & Egg Skins

10 large potato skins, lightly crisped

2 cups each diced smoked ham and diced cheddar cheese
4 hard-cooked eggs, chopped
2 scallions, minced
¼ cup each chopped black olives and green bell peppers
¾ cup mayonnaise
½ teaspoon prepared mustard
Seasoned salt and black pepper to taste

10 slices cheddar cheese

Garnish { paprika
         { green bell pepper rings

🫑 Preheat oven to 375°. Combine ham with remaining ingre~dients except sliced cheddar and garnish. Fill skins. Place a slice of cheddar on top of each skin, cutting to fit evenly.

🫑 Bake skins about 20 minutes, or until heated through and cheese is melted.

🫑 To serve: Sprinkle tops lightly with paprika, and place a green pepper ring in the center of each skin.

Makes 10 large skins.

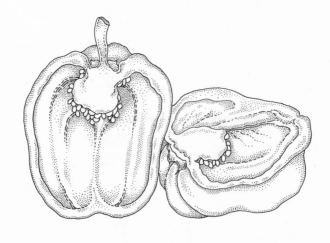

Knockwurst & Sauerkraut Skins

6 large potato skins, crisped or fried

½ cup sour cream
1 scallion, minced
1 teaspoon prepared spicy mustard
½ teaspoon horseradish
⅛ teaspoon salt

6 oz. Jack cheese, thinly sliced
6 knockwurst, cooked and hot
1 8-oz. can sauerkraut, heated

Garnish {paprika

- In a small bowl, combine sour cream, scallion, mustard, horseradish and salt; set aside.

- Into each skin, lay an equal amount of sliced cheese. Broil briefly, just until cheese melts.

- To serve: Place a hot knockwurst into each cheese~filled skin and top it with a helping of drained sauerkraut. Generously spoon on the sour cream sauce. Sprinkle tops lightly with paprika.

Makes 6 large skins.

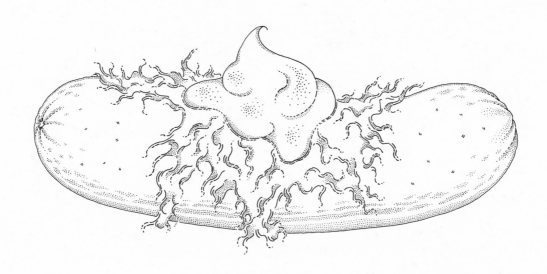

Cheesy Crab Melt Skins

6 to 8 large potato skins, lightly crisped

3/4 lb. cooked and flaked crab meat

1 cup shredded Jack cheese

2 scallions, minced

1/4 cup diced celery

4 oz. cream cheese, softened

1/4 cup mayonnaise

2 teaspoons lemon juice

Salt and pepper to taste

6 to 8 slices Jack cheese

Topping { 1 medium-size tomato, thinly sliced
         { grated Parmesan cheese

Garnish { chopped fresh parsley

◈ Preheat oven to 375.° In a mixing bowl, combine crab with shredded Jack, scallions and celery. In a small bowl, blend cream cheese, mayonnaise, lemon juice, salt and pepper until smooth. Stir into crab mixture, mixing well.

◈ Stuff skins with crab filling. Place a cheese slice over each. Bake about 20 minutes, or until hot and cheese is melted.

◈ Place a slice of tomato atop each skin and sprinkle with Parmesan. Broil until surfaces are golden brown. Garnish with parsley.

Makes 6 to 8 large skins.

Barbecued Beef Skins

6 large potato skins, crisped or fried and hot

1½ lbs. beef stew meat

1 large green bell pepper, chopped

1 large onion, diced

2 cloves garlic, crushed

2 8-oz. cans tomato sauce

¼ cup each vinegar, honey and dark brown sugar

3 tablespoons Worcestershire sauce

2 teaspoons dry mustard

1 teaspoon each salt and chili powder

Tabasco to taste

~Shredded lettuce, cabbage, or coleslaw~

Garnishes { chopped sweet onion
sliced black olives
chopped tomato
corn chips

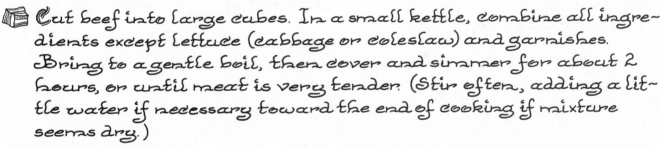

Cut beef into large cubes. In a small kettle, combine all ingredients except lettuce (cabbage or coleslaw) and garnishes. Bring to a gentle boil, then cover and simmer for about 2 hours, or until meat is very tender. (Stir often, adding a little water if necessary toward the end of cooking if mixture seems dry.)

You may leave the meat in chunks, or pull it into shreds with two forks.

Into each skin, place some lettuce. Top with a helping of meat mixture, and garnish with one or more of the suggestions above.

Makes 6 large skins.

Chili Dog Skins

Serve hot, with pickle spears and fresh fruit.

6 large potato skins, crisped or fried and hot
6 hot dogs
1 15-oz. can chili and beans
1 cup shredded cheddar cheese

Topping & Garnish { ½ cup diced onion
corn chips

- Make a few diagonal slashes on the surface of each hot dog. Bake, boil, or broil them until hot. Place each one in a potato skin.
- Meanwhile, heat the chili and beans in a small saucepan. Spoon about 2 heaping tablespoons around each hot dog. Sprinkle the tops with cheddar cheese.
- Broil the skins until cheese melts nicely. Garnish each with onions and corn chips.

Makes 6 large skins.

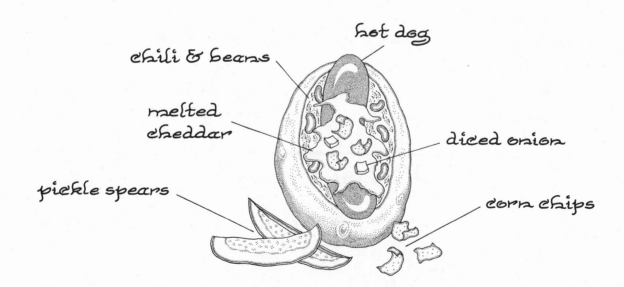

hot dog

chili & beans

melted cheddar

diced onion

pickle spears

corn chips

BLT Skins with Cheese

6 large potato skins, crisped or fried

6 slices of your favorite cheese (cheddar, Jack, Swiss, etc.)
6 crisp lettuce leaves
Mayonnaise
2 medium~size tomatoes, thinly sliced
9 slices bacon, crisply cooked and broken in half

Garnish {sliced black olives

Place a cheese slice (cutting to fit) on each skin. Broil until melted. Lay a lettuce leaf on top, then spread generously with mayonnaise. Place approximately 2 tomato slices over the top, followed by 3 bacon halves. Sprinkle with olives and serve.

Makes 6 large skins.

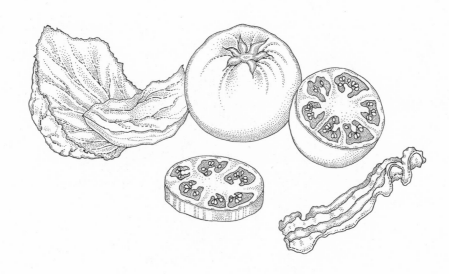

Avocado & Sprout Skins

Healthfully easy.

6 large potato skins, crisped or fried
6 slices Jack, Swiss, or Muenster cheese
Mayonnaise
Alfalfa sprouts (about 1 packed cup)
1 large avocado, thinly sliced
6 slices bacon, crisply cooked and crumbled

Garnish (sunflower seeds, raw or toasted

Place a slice of cheese on each skin (cutting to fit) and broil until melted. Spread with mayonnaise. Top with a nice helping of sprouts. Lay on some avocado slices and sprinkle with bacon. Garnish tops with sunflower seeds. Pass extra seeds for munching.

Makes 6 large skins.

Note: For a vegetarian dish, substitute soy bacon bits.

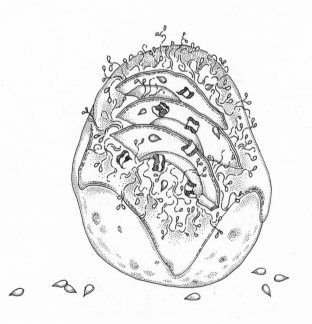

54

Creamy Tuna Melt Skins

Hot and cheesy!

6 large potato skins, lightly crisped

2 6½-oz. cans tuna, drained
1 cup shredded cheddar cheese
2 scallions, minced
1 stalk celery, diced
¼ cup sweet pickle relish
¼ teaspoon seasoned salt
Fresh black pepper
Dash of dill weed

4 oz. cream cheese, softened
2 tablespoons milk or cream

Topping { 2 medium-size tomatoes, thinly sliced
¾ cup packed shredded cheddar cheese
grated Parmesan cheese

Garnish { chopped parsley

1. Preheat oven to 375°. In a large bowl, flake tuna. Stir in 1 cup cheddar, the scallions, celery, relish and seasonings. In a small bowl, mix cream cheese with milk until smooth. Thoroughly blend into tuna mixture.

2. Place the skins on a baking tray, and fill them solidly with the tuna mixture. Cover securely with foil. Bake for 20 minutes, or until hot. Uncover the skins. Lay tomato slices on top, and sprinkle with the remaining cheddar. Dust lightly with Parmesan.

3. Broil until cheese is melted and golden. Garnish each skin with parsley.

Makes 6 large skins.

Hot Reuben Skins

6 large potato skins, lightly crisped

Thousand Island Dressing:

½ cup mayonnaise
1 tablespoon <u>each</u> chili sauce, chopped pimento~stuffed olives,
   grated onion and sweet pickle relish (drained)

3 to 4 oz. cooked corned beef, very thinly sliced
1 8~oz. can sauerkraut, drained
Caraway seeds
6 slices Swiss cheese
1 large tomato, seeded and chopped

Garnish { Thousand Island Dressing
          paprika

Prepare dressing: In a small bowl, mix together mayonnaise, chili sauce, olives, onion and relish. Chill a few hours to height~en flavor.

Preheat oven to 350° Spoon a little of the dressing evenly into each potato cavity. Top with slices of corned beef and a help~ing of sauerkraut. Sprinkle lightly with caraway seeds. Lay cheese slices on top (cutting them to fit), and sprinkle with the chopped tomato.

Cover the skins securely with foil. Bake about 20 minutes, or until thoroughly hot and cheese melts. Spoon some dressing on top of each skin, followed by a light dusting of paprika. Pass any extra dressing.

Makes 6 large skins.

56

Sicilian Sausage Sub Skins

Serve with a leafy green salad laced with oil and vinegar.

6 large potato skins, crisped or fried and _hot_

1 lb. Italian sweet sausage, formed into 1-inch balls

1 medium-size onion, cut into thin wedges

1 _each_ red and green bell peppers, cut into strips

1 clove garlic, crushed

A handful of small mushrooms, halved

¼ cup chopped pimento

½ teaspoon basil

¼ teaspoon oregano

Salt and pepper to taste

Topping
{
2 tablespoons grated Parmesan cheese
1 cup shredded mozzarella cheese
1 medium-size tomato, seeded and chopped
¼ cup sliced black olives
}

Garnish
{
6 pickled Italian peppers
6 parsley sprigs
}

In a medium-size skillet, brown sausage balls over low heat on all sides until thoroughly cooked; remove to paper towels to drain. In drippings, sauté onion, peppers, garlic and mushrooms until just tender. Add pimento, seasonings, and cooked sausage balls. Simmer a minute or two to blend flavors.

In each potato skin, spoon on some of the sautéed vegetables. Top with sausage balls, then Parmesan. Heap on the mozzarella, tomatoes and olives.

Broil until mozzarella is melted and all is hot. Top each skin with a pickled pepper and parsley sprig.

Makes 6 large skins.

Note on Potato Skin Etiquette: You are allowed to eat these with your hands! Pass the napkins, and enjoy yourself.

Hot Cashew Chicken Melt Skins

5 large potato skins, crisped or fried

2 cups finely diced cooked chicken
½ cup lightly toasted cashew pieces
⅓ cup diagonally sliced celery
¼ cup each diced green bell peppers and water chestnuts
1 scallion, thinly sliced
½ cup mayonnaise (more if needed)
2 teaspoons each soy sauce and lemon juice
Salt and pepper to taste
5 slices cheddar cheese

Garnish { whole cashew pieces
         { finely shredded lettuce

- Preheat oven to 350°. Mix chicken with all the remaining ingredients except cheddar cheese and garnish. Pile into skins.

- Top each filled skin with a cheese slice, cutting to fit. Bake on a cookie sheet for about 20 minutes, or until everything is hot and cheese is soft and gooey.

- Serve the "melts" hot, garnished with whole cashews on a bed of shredded lettuce.

Makes 5 large skins

Monte Cristo Skins

Ham, cheese and chicken baked inside a sweet custard.

8 large potato skins, lightly crisped

8 long, thin slices boiled ham (about 12 oz.)
8 thin slices Swiss cheese (about ½ lb.)
1 cup chopped cooked chicken

3 eggs
¾ cup half-and-half
1 tablespoon sugar
¼ teaspoon salt

Garnish {powdered sugar

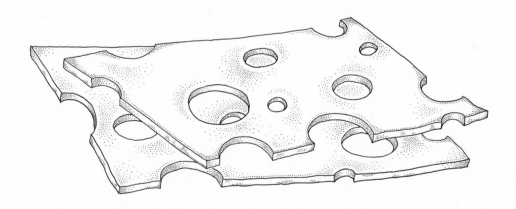

Preheat oven to 375°. On each slice of ham, place 1 slice of Swiss cheese and approximately 2 tablespoons of chicken. Roll up. Place a stuffed ham slice into each skin and lay them on a shallow baking tray.

In a small bowl, beat eggs with half-and-half, sugar and salt. Carefully pour this custard into each skin.

Bake for 30 to 35 minutes, or until the custard is just set. Broil skins until golden brown on top. Sprinkle with powdered sugar and serve.

Makes 8 large skins.

Eggs and Cheese Skins

Here we have an unbeatable pair. The concoctions you can create with eggs and cheese are virtually limitless, especially if you also combine them with fresh vegetables, herbs, and possibly a bit of meat here and there. In this chapter, you will encounter a splendid array of recipes from Elegant Eggs Benedict Skins to Creamy Curried Egg Skins to a delightful assortment of Quiche Skins (egg custard fillings baked inside a crispy potato "shell"—mmmm!) The recipes in this section are wonderful for brunches, too. So why not plan a get-together with family or friends for this coming weekend and serve any one of these masterpieces? You'll all be in potato heaven!

Asparagus & Egg Skins with Sour Cream Cheese Sauce

Perfect for a Sunday brunch in springtime with good friends.

16 large potato skins, crisped or fried

1½ lbs. fresh young asparagus, steamed just until tender (keep warm)

8 hard-cooked eggs, neatly sliced

¼ cup butter	2 teaspoons dry mustard
½ cup minced onion	1 teaspoon Worcestershire sauce
1 clove garlic, crushed	½ teaspoon seasoned salt
¼ cup flour	Fresh black pepper
2 cups half-and-half	Dash of Tabasco
2 cups grated cheddar cheese	½ cup sour cream

Topping { ½ cup grated cheddar

Garnish { chopped fresh parsley

- Melt butter in a large saucepan; sauté onion and garlic until translucent. Remove from heat and blend in flour. Slowly stir in half-and-half to avoid lumping. Stir mixture over medium heat until sauce starts to bubble. Stir a minute longer, then remove from heat and blend in 2 cups cheddar along with mustard, Worcestershire, salt, pepper and Tabasco. Set sauce aside.

- In each skin, lay pieces of asparagus lengthwise to cover bottom. (You'll have to cut the spears to fit.) Top with egg slices, slightly overlapping.

- Stir sour cream into cheese sauce. Carefully spoon sauce over eggs and asparagus, filling each skin as generously as possible.

- Sprinkle remaining ½ cup cheddar over the tops. Broil or bake at 350° until cheese melts and all is uniformly hot.

- Lastly, sprinkle on some fresh parsley and serve.

Makes 16 large skins.

Egg Skins Florentine

Frozen spinach makes this sophisticated dish quite easy.

8 large potato skins, crisped or fried and <u>hot</u>

2 10-oz. packages frozen chopped spinach
3 tablespoons butter
3 tablespoons flour
2 cups half-and-half, warmed
½ teaspoon salt
A few dashes <u>each</u> nutmeg and cayenne
1 cup packed shredded Swiss cheese
Dash of dry sherry

8 eggs

Topping { ¼ cup grated Parmesan cheese
          paprika

Garnish { freshly chopped parsley

Cook spinach as directed on package; drain well and squeeze out all excess liquid. Cover and keep warm.

Make cheese sauce: Melt butter in a medium-size saucepan. Whisk in the flour until smooth. Remove pan from heat and gradually blend in half-and-half, salt, nutmeg and cayenne until smooth. Return pan to medium-low heat, whisking continually until sauce thickens and boils for a couple of minutes. Stir in Swiss cheese to melt, then a dash of sherry.

Mix 1 generous cup of sauce with the drained and still warm spinach. Cover both the plain sauce and the spinach mixture to keep them each hot while you proceed with the next step.

Now, poach the eggs to desired firmness (about 3 to 5 minutes in a large skillet containing 1½ to 2 inches of boiling water).

To assemble: Spread an even layer of spinach mixture in each skin. Top each with a well drained, perfectly poached egg, and a generous spoonful of the remaining plain cheese sauce. Dust paprika over the tops.

 Broil just until tops turn golden brown, watching diligently. Sprinkle with parsley before serving.

Makes 8 large skins.

Elegant Eggs Benedict Skins

4 large potato skins, crisped or fried and hot
½ cup (1 stick) butter
3 egg yolks
2 teaspoons lemon juice
Dash or two of cayenne
4 to 8 slices Canadian bacon
4 whole eggs
~Paprika~

Make Hollandaise Sauce: Melt the butter in a small saucepan until bubbly. In a blender, combine the egg yolks, lemon juice and cayenne until well mixed. Remove the center cover of the blender and add the hot melted butter in a very slow stream, blending on low until nice and thick. Cover and keep warm.

Poach the 4 whole eggs and lightly sauté the bacon slices until hot.

To assemble: Place 1 or 2 bacon slices on each skin. Top with a drained poached egg, then some Hollandaise Sauce. Dust with paprika, and serve promptly.

Makes 4 large skins.

Creamy Curried Egg Skins

Tastes as good as it smells.

8 large potato skins, crisped or fried and hot

¼ cup butter
¼ cup minced onion
1 small clove garlic, crushed
¼ teaspoon grated fresh ginger
1 small sweet red pepper, diced
1 small tart green apple,
　cored, peeled and chopped
1 teaspoon curry powder
¼ teaspoon salt
Pinch finely grated lemon peel

½ cup raisins
¼ cup flour
1 cup chicken stock
½ cup half~and~half
½ cup yogurt
4 slices bacon, cooked and
　crumbled
5 hard~cooked eggs, peeled
　and chopped

Garnish { ¼ cup shredded coconut
{ ¼ cup chopped toasted peanuts

Heat butter in a large saucepan and sauté onion, garlic, ginger, red pepper, apple, curry and salt together until pepper and apple soften and become just~tender. Add lemon peel and raisins and cook a minute or two longer.

Remove pan from heat and blend in flour. Gradually add stock, then half~and~half, stirring until smooth. Return pan to heat and simmer, stirring faithfully until sauce thickens and bubbles.

Over low heat, stir in yogurt, bacon and eggs. Heat very gently until hot, but don't allow sauce to boil.

Fill skins with curried egg mixture. Combine coconut and peanuts and sprinkle lavishly over the tops. Serve prompt~ly!

Makes 8 large skins.

Mushroom Scrambled Egg Skins Baked in Cheddar Sauce

Treat yourself (and loved ones) to this recipe.

12 large potato skins, lightly crisped
¼ cup butter
1 clove garlic, crushed
½ cup diced onion
1 cup chopped mushrooms
12 eggs, well beaten

¼ cup butter
¼ cup flour
2 cups half-and-half or milk
1 cup packed grated sharp cheddar cheese
¼ cup diced pimento
¼ cup crumbled cooked bacon, diced ham or thinly sliced hot dogs
2 tablespoons chopped parsley
½ teaspoon each salt and dry mustard
Fresh black pepper

Topping {
1 cup soft fresh bread crumbs
½ cup grated Parmesan cheese
2 tablespoons melted butter
2 medium-size tomatoes, cut into 12 thin slices

Garnish {fresh chopped parsley

⊙ Melt ¼ cup butter in a large skillet and sauté garlic, onion and mushrooms until just tender. Pour in beaten eggs and scramble over medium heat until set. Remove skillet from heat and set aside.

⊙ Preheat oven to 350°. In a large saucepan, melt ¼ cup butter. Blend in flour until smooth. Over low heat, slowly whisk in half-and-half. Bring sauce to a boil, stirring constantly, until thick. Continue to stir and simmer for an additional minute. Blend in cheddar, then remove from heat. Fold in pimento, bacon, 2 tablespoons parsley, seasonings, and your eagerly awaiting scrambled eggs — combine gently but thoroughly.

⊛ Fill skins with egg mixture. Combine bread crumbs, Parmesan and 2 tablespoons melted butter. Sprinkle most of this crumb mixture evenly over the skins. Place 1 tomato slice upon the crumbs, then sprinkle with remaining crumb mixture.

⊛ Bake skins on a buttered tray for about 25 minutes. Top with fresh chopped parsley to serve.

Makes 12 large skins.

Egg Skins Foo Young

Potato skins — the Chinese way.

8 large potato skins, lightly crisped

8 eggs
6 tablespoons cold water
2 tablespoons cornstarch
1 tablespoon soy sauce
½ teaspoon Chinese sesame oil
Salt and pepper to taste

1½ cups bean sprouts
1 cup thinly sliced mushrooms
½ cup thinly sliced scallions
   (reserve greens for garnish)
½ cup each sliced Chinese pea
   pods and chopped water chestnuts
2 tablespoons oil

Topping {very lightly toasted sesame seeds
Garnish {reserved scallion greens

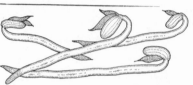

- Preheat oven to 350°. In a large bowl, beat eggs with cold water until combined. Whisk in cornstarch, soy sauce, sesame oil, salt and pepper until well blended. (You may have to put this through a strainer to rid yourself of any lumps.) Set egg mixture aside.

- In a skillet, sauté bean sprouts, mushrooms, scallions (whites only), pea pods and water chestnuts in hot oil until crisp~tender. Evenly divide sautéed veggies into each potato skin. Ladle on the egg mixture, filling to the rims. Sprinkle tops with sesame seeds.

- Bake 20 to 25 minutes, or until most of the filling is set, but surfaces are still moist. Broil skins briefly, until tops just turn golden brown and eggs are firm.

- Garnish with reserved sliced scallion greens and serve with extra soy sauce.

Makes 8 large skins.

Tip: Make sure the skins are free of holes and tears.

Ricotta Frittata Skins

In Italian-style omelette baked inside crispy skins.

6 to 8 large potato skins, lightly crisped

1 tablespoon butter
1 heaping cup thinly sliced zucchini
½ cup minced onion
1 small clove garlic, finely minced
¼ teaspoon basil

4 eggs
1 cup ricotta cheese
3 tablespoons Parmesan or Romano cheese
1 tablespoon chopped parsley
Salt and freshly ground black pepper to taste

Topping & Garnish { melted butter
extra Parmesan or Romano

Preheat oven to 350°. In a medium-size skillet, melt 1 tablespoon butter and sauté zucchini with onion, garlic and basil until vegetables are very tender but not brown, set aside.

In a bowl, beat eggs with a wire whisk until frothy. Beat in ricotta, Parmesan or Romano, parsley, salt and pepper until mixture is smooth and creamy. Stir in the sautéed veggies.

Fill the skins to the top with the egg/zucchini mixture. Bake for about 20 minutes, or until eggs are almost firm and still a bit moist. Brush surfaces lightly with melted butter and sprinkle with extra Parmesan. Broil until tops turn golden brown and puff up slightly. Serve right away.

Makes 6 to 8 large skins.

Alternative approach: Instead of the melted butter and Parmesan topping, lay very thin slices of Mozzarella cheese atop each skin and broil until melted and gooey. Top with more parsley and even some sliced olives.

Baked Egg Skins, Western~Style

Petite egg casseroles garnished with fresh tomatoes and a savory crumb topping.

10 to 12 large potato skins, lightly crisped

8 eggs

6 tablespoons sour cream, room temperature

2 tablespoons butter

½ cup each minced onion and diced ham

½ cup each chopped green bell peppers and diced cooked potatoes

1 small clove garlic, crushed (optional)

½ teaspoon seasoned salt

Fresh black pepper

A dash or 2 of cayenne

¾ cup grated Jack or cheddar cheese

~Paprika~

Topping & Garnish
{
1 cup seeded and diced tomatoes
½ cup soft bread crumbs
¼ cup grated Parmesan cheese
1 tablespoon melted butter
}

Preheat oven to 375°. In a large bowl, beat eggs with sour cream until well blended; set aside.

Melt butter in a large skillet; sauté onion, ham, green peppers, potatoes and garlic together until onion is tender and flavors mingle. Add the sauté to the beaten egg mixture and season with salt, pepper and cayenne.

Place the already crisped skins on a large flat baking tray (make certain they are free from holes or tears) and pour egg mixture evenly into each. Be sure to distribute the solids evenly, too. Sprinkle each skin with its share of Jack or cheddar, and dust with paprika.

Bake skins for 15 to 20 minutes, or until eggs are set and

cheese is melted (a knife inserted should come out clean). Remove tray from oven and turn the temperature up to "broil." Cover each skin with some chopped tomatoes. In a small bowl, toss bread crumbs with Parmesan and melted butter. Sprinkle crumb mixture generously over tomatoes.

Broil skins until crumbs brown lightly and egg filling starts to puff up. Serve immediately!

Makes 10 to 12 large skins.

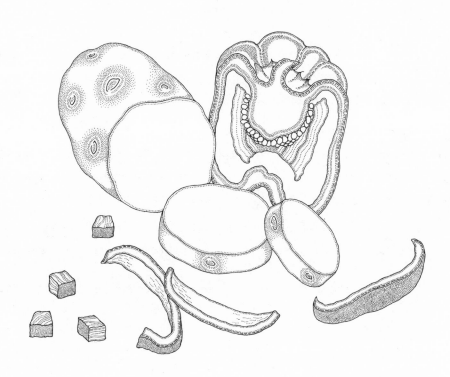

Egg & Mushroom Skins au Gratin

6 medium~size potato skins, lightly crisped

2 to 3 tablespoons butter
2 scallions (thinly slice whites, mince greens and reserve)
2 generous cups thinly sliced mushrooms
Optional ~ 1 small clove garlic, minced

6 eggs
Seasoned salt and fresh black pepper
6 tablespoons half~and~half
½ cup packed grated Swiss cheese

Garnish { crumbled cooked bacon or soy bacon bits
         { minced scallion greens

◎ Preheat oven to 325°. Melt butter in a medium~size skillet. Sauté scallions (whites only), mushrooms and the optional garlic until tender but not mushy.

◎ Place an equal portion of the sautéed vegetables in each potato skin. Carefully break an egg into each, then sprinkle to taste with seasoned salt and pepper. Top each egg with 1 tablespoon of half~and~half and some grated cheese.

◎ Bake skins for about 20 minutes, or until eggs are just set. Top with bacon and reserved scallion greens to serve.

Makes 6 medium~size skins ~ recipe easily doubled.

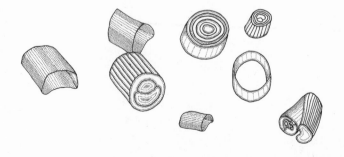

Cheddar & Chili Soufflé Skins

Garnishing is optional, these look so gorgeous.

10 large potato skins, lightly crisped

6 eggs, separated, and at room temperature

3 tablespoons butter

2 scallions, minced (whites and greens)

3 tablespoons flour

1 cup half-and-half or milk

¼ cup sour cream, room temperature

1½ cups packed grated sharp cheddar cheese.

1 teaspoon spicy brown mustard

½ teaspoon seasoned salt

A dash or 2 of cayenne

2 to 4 tablespoons chopped canned green chilies, drained

Optional Garnishes {
small spoonfuls of sour cream
a dusting of paprika
a ripe olive atop each
}

❧ Melt butter in a medium-size saucepan and sauté scallions until soft. Slowly sprinkle in the flour, stirring constantly over low heat. Remove pan from heat and gradually blend in half-and-half or milk, stirring as you pour. Return pan to heat and bring to a gentle boil. Boil and stir for 1 to 2 minutes, or until sauce is quite thick. Remove from heat and add sour cream and cheddar all at once, blending until cheese melts and mixture is thick and smooth. Stir in mustard, salt, cayenne and chilies. Cool sauce until lukewarm.

❧ Meanwhile, preheat oven to 375°. In a small bowl, beat egg yolks. Beat them well into the lukewarm sauce and set aside. In a large bowl, beat egg whites until stiff. Gently but thoroughly fold egg whites into sauce mixture.

❧ Promptly fill skins to slightly rounded tops (they will rise) and bake without interruption for 15 to 20 minutes, or until tops have risen and browned sufficiently. Serve immediately, garnished or not.

Makes 10 large skins.

Creamy Scrambled Egg & Liver Skins

Certain to be a hit at your next brunch.

6 to 7 large potato skins, crisped or fried and hot

1 tablespoon butter
½ cup chopped onion
¼ cup minced green bell pepper
½ lb. chicken livers, cut into chunks
1 teaspoon Worcestershire sauce
Salt and pepper

1 tablespoon butter
7 eggs
¼ cup milk
½ teaspoon salt
¼ teaspoon tarragon
Fresh black pepper
1 3-oz. package cream cheese, cut into cubes

Garnish {paprika
{6 or 7 parsley sprigs

Melt 1 tablespoon butter in a medium-size skillet; briefly sauté onion and green pepper. Add the livers, and sauté everything together until the livers are cooked. Stir in the Worcestershire and season lightly with salt and pepper. Remove liver mixture to a bowl and set aside.

Wipe the skillet clean and melt the remaining tablespoon of butter until it sizzles. Beat together the eggs, milk, ½ teaspoon salt, tarragon and pepper; pour into skillet. Scramble gently by folding the eggs as they cook. When eggs are softly set, stir in the cream cheese and continue to fold until eggs are cooked but still moist and creamy. Fold in the livers and heat briefly.

Pile the egg mixture into the skins. Sprinkle the tops lightly with paprika, and garnish each with a parsley sprig.

Makes 6 to 7 large skins.

Cheesy Potato Pancake Skins

Accompany with scrambled eggs, warm spiced applesauce, and freshly brewed coffee.

10 to 12 large potato skins, lightly crisped

1 8~oz. package cream cheese, softened
2 eggs
3 tablespoons flour
¾ teaspoon salt
¼ teaspoon caraway seeds
Fresh black pepper
Dash nutmeg

¼ cup finely minced onion
1 cup diced smoked ham
2 cups grated Swiss cheese
4 cups packed shredded cooked potatoes

~Paprika~
~Melted butter~

Garnish {chopped fresh parsley

- Preheat oven to 375.° In a large bowl, beat cream cheese with eggs, flour, salt and seasonings until smooth. Blend in onion, ham, Swiss cheese and potatoes until well combined.

- Pack an even amount of potato mixture into each skin. Sprinkle surfaces lightly with paprika.

- Bake for 30 minutes. Remove skins from the oven and gently brush them with melted butter. Bake them for an additional 10 minutes, then broil them briefly until the surfaces are brown and crisp. Serve at once, garnished with chopped parsley.

Makes 10 to 12 large skins.

Cheesy Mexican Egg Skins

Serve with sliced bacon, fresh fruit and a large pitcher of Margaritas, and you'll be halfway to the border!

8 large potato skins, crisped or fried and hot

12 eggs
½ cup half-and-half
½ teaspoon seasoned salt
¼ teaspoon each oregano and
    cumin
Fresh black pepper

2 tablespoons butter
2 scallions, finely chopped
1 large clove garlic, crushed
¼ cup chopped canned green
    chilies
¼ cup sliced black olives
1 cup Jack cheese, cut into
    small cubes.

Topping
    &
Garnish
{ paprika
{ dollops of sour cream
{ 1 perfectly ripe avocado, peeled and cut into 8 slices

In a large mixing bowl, whisk together eggs, half-and-half, seasoned salt, oregano, cumin and black pepper until all is well blended; set aside.

In a heavy skillet, melt butter. Sauté scallions and garlic in butter until soft. Pour in egg mixture. Cook over medium-low heat until eggs are almost set, gently stirring every so often. When eggs are still moist, stir in chilies, olives and cheese. With a light touch, fold mixture together until cheese melts and eggs are done to your personal preference. (You may wish to cover the skillet for a minute or so to melt the cheese further — use very low heat.

Fill the skins artfully with the scrambled egg mixture. Sprinkle with paprika and top with a dollop of sour cream. Crown with an avocado slice and serve pronto.

Makes 8 large skins.

Swiss Cauliflower
& Broccoli Skins au Gratin

Delicious brunch fare! Serve with a simple egg dish and a fresh fruit salad.

14 large potato skins, crisped or fried

¾ lb. _each_ fresh broccoli and cauliflower — trimmed, broken into bite~size pieces and steamed just until tender. (That's 1½ lbs. total veggies!)

5 slices bacon, chopped
1 medium~size onion, diced
⅓ cup minced green bell pepper
3 tablespoons flour
1 cup _plus_ 2 tablespoons half~and~half
¾ cup chicken stock

¾ teaspoon salt
Fresh black pepper
1 cup grated Swiss cheese
2 ½ teaspoons dry sherry
1 large firm~ripe tomato, seeded and coarsely chopped

Topping { ½ cup fresh bread crumbs (sourdough is nice)
2 tablespoons _each_ melted butter and Parmesan cheese

Keep broccoli and cauliflower warm, or better yet, steam them while you prepare the sauce.

In a medium~size saucepan, cook bacon with onion and bell pepper until all is tender. Remove from heat and blend in flour. Slowly stir in half~and~half and stock until smooth. Add seasonings. Return pan to heat and bring mixture to a gentle boil, stirring. Boil for 1 minute. Remove from heat and add Swiss cheese and sherry.

Drain the broccoli and cauliflower, and combine it with the cheese sauce. Stir in tomato. Spoon vegetable mixture generously into each skin. For topping, combine crumbs with melted butter and Parmesan. Sprinkle over tops.

Broil until crumbs begin to brown and skins are hot. Watch closely.

Makes 14 large skins.

Welsh Rarebit Skins

Crunchy potato skins, crispy bacon, and fresh tomato slices bathed in a rich and filling cheese sauce.

8 large potato skins, crisped or fried and hot
¼ cup butter
1 clove garlic, finely minced
¼ cup flour
½ teaspoon each salt, dry mustard, and Worcestershire sauce
Fresh black pepper
¾ cup each milk and beer
2 cups shredded sharp cheddar cheese
Tabasco sauce to taste

2 medium-size tomatoes, sliced
8 slices bacon, cooked and halved crosswise

Garnish { 8 parsley sprigs

Melt butter in a medium-size saucepan and sauté garlic lightly. Blend in flour, salt, mustard, Worcestershire, and pepper. Remove from heat and gradually add the milk and beer and stir until smooth.

Cook over low heat, stirring constantly, until sauce thickens and boils. Boil and stir a minute longer. Blend in the cheese and Tabasco.

Using about ½ of the sauce, spoon some into each skin. Lay tomato slices on top of the sauce, then place 2 bacon halves in a criss-cross pattern over the tomatoes. Spoon the remaining sauce over all

Broil until the cheese sauce turns golden brown on top. Garnish each skin with a parsley sprig. Serve hot.

Makes 8 large skins.

Country Breakfast Skins

Hearty and filling. Perfect for a crowd of hungry folk.

12 large potato skins, lightly crisped

2 tablespoons butter
8 scallions (whites sliced,
   greens minced and reserved
2 cups *each* diced cooked potato
   and diced smoked ham
Seasoned salt and black pepper

Sauce:

¼ cup butter
¼ cup flour
¾ teaspoon seasoned salt
Fresh black pepper
2 cups *each* chicken stock and
   sour cream
2 tablespoons minced parsley

8 hard-cooked eggs, sliced

Garnish { paprika
          reserved scallion greens

◎ Preheat oven to 350°. Melt 2 tablespoons butter in a medium-size skillet. Sauté scallion whites with potato and ham until onions are soft and potatoes lightly browned. Sprinkle with seasoned salt and pepper to taste. Set aside.

◎ Make sauce: Melt ¼ cup butter in a medium-size saucepan. Remove from heat and blend in flour, ¾ teaspoon seasoned salt and black pepper. Gradually add chicken stock, stirring until smooth. Cook over low heat until mixture comes to a boil. Boil and stir 1 minute longer. Slowly blend the hot sauce into the sour cream along with the parsley.

◎ To assemble: Place the skins side by side in a large, shallow baking dish. Divide the potato-ham mixture evenly into each skin. Lay a few neatly overlapping egg slices on top, then generously pour on the warm sauce.

◎ Bake, uncovered, for 10 to 15 minutes, or until thoroughly hot. To serve, dust the tops lightly with paprika and sprinkle with the reserved scallion greens.

Make 12 large skins.

Cheese & Raisin Blintz Skins

6 large potato skins, lightly crisped

2 cups ricotta cheese

2 tablespoons sugar

1 egg yolk

½ teaspoon vanilla

½ cup dark or golden raisins

Topping { 1 tablespoon sugar
           ½ teaspoon cinnamon

Melted butter

Garnish { sour cream
          chunky applesauce
          your favorite stewed fruit or compote

Preheat oven to 350°. In a large bowl, beat ricotta cheese with 2 tablespoons sugar, the egg yolk and vanilla until well blended. Stir in the raisins.

Fill each skin to the rim with the cheese mixture, making the tops smooth and even. Thoroughly mix together 1 tablespoon sugar and the cinnamon. Sprinkle ½ of this cinnamon~sugar over the surfaces of the skins.

Bake, uncovered, for 30 minutes. Drizzle or lightly brush the tops with melted butter, then broil briefly until golden brown on top. Sprinkle with the remaining cinnamon~sugar mixture, and serve with any or all of the above garnishes.

Makes 6 large skins.

Dexter

Myrtle

Herman

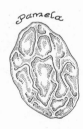
Pamela

Scrambled Crab & Artichoke Skins

8 large potato skins, crisped or fried and hot

1 tablespoon butter
2 large scallions, thinly sliced
1 clove garlic, crushed
1 heaping cup sliced mushrooms
1 cup marinated artichoke hearts,
    drained and cut into pieces
1 cup flaked cooked crab meat
1 tablespoon butter

8 eggs
¼ cup half-and-half
½ teaspoon seasoned salt
¼ teaspoon basil
Fresh black pepper
1 3-oz. package cream cheese,
    cut into cubes
½ cup shredded Jack cheese

Topping { ½ cup shredded Jack cheese
         { grated Parmesan

Garnish { paprika

Melt 1 tablespoon butter in a large skillet and sauté scallions, garlic and mushrooms until tender. Fold in artichoke hearts and crab, and sauté lightly for a minute or two. Remove the vegetable mixture to a bowl.

In the same skillet, heat the remaining tablespoon of butter. In a bowl, beat eggs with half-and-half, seasoned salt, basil and pepper; pour into skillet. Scramble gently by folding the eggs as they set. While still moist, blend in the cream cheese and ½ cup Jack until cheeses are melted and creamy. Fold in the vegetable~crab mixture until everything is nicely mingled.

Spoon the egg mixture into the hot skins. Top each with some of the remaining Jack cheese, and sprinkle lightly with Parmesan.

Broil until cheese melts. Dust with paprika before serving.

Makes 8 large skins.

Green Eggs & Ham Skins

6 large potato skins, crisped or fried and hot

1 tablespoon butter
2 scallions, thinly sliced
2 tablespoons each minced green pepper and celery
1 small clove garlic, crushed
½ cup diced smoked ham

8 eggs
¼ cup heavy (whipping) cream
2 tablespoons chopped fresh parsley
¼ teaspoon each seasoned salt and basil
Fresh black pepper
⅔ cup packed shredded Jack cheese

Topping & Garnish {
1 medium-size tomato, seeded and chopped
paprika

Melt butter in a large, heavy skillet. Sauté scallions with green pepper, celery, garlic and ham until veggies are just-tender, stirring often.

In a large mixing bowl, beat eggs with cream, parsley, seasoned salt, basil and pepper until well combined. Pour egg mixture into skillet. Scramble everything together lightly by folding gently as the eggs set with a rubber spatula or wooden spoon. When eggs are almost done, blend in the cheese and continue to fold until cheese melts and eggs are cooked but still moist.

Pile the egg mixture into the skins, filling generously. Place some chopped tomatoes in the center of each skin, followed by a thorough dusting of paprika. Serve hot.

Makes 6 large skins.

Huevos Rancheros Skins

6 very large potato skins, crisped or fried and <u>hot</u>

3 slices bacon, diced
1 medium-size onion, chopped
1 small green pepper, chopped
1 clove garlic, crushed
2 cups chopped ripe tomatoes
1/3 cup diced green chilies
1/2 teaspoon cumin
Salt and pepper to taste

6 eggs
Oil for frying
More salt and pepper

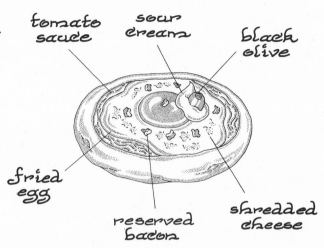

tomato sauce

sour cream

black olive

fried egg

reserved bacon

shredded cheese

Garnish { 3/4 cup finely shredded Jack or cheddar cheese
sour cream
reserved bacon
6 whole pitted black olives

Fry bacon in a medium-size skillet until crisp; remove bacon to paper towels. In drippings, sauté onion, green pepper and garlic until tender. Stir in tomatoes, chilies, cumin, salt and pepper. Heat gently to boiling, then simmer for 10 to 15 minutes, or until sauce thickens.

A few minutes before the sauce is done, prepare the eggs: You can poach them in an egg poacher for uniform roundness, or fry them very gently in 1/8 inch oil heated in a large skillet. Cook them sunny side up. Season with more salt and pepper, if you like.

Into each skin, spoon a tablespoon of sauce, then carefully top with a cooked egg (you may need to trim some of the whites to fit). Surround the eggs with remaining sauce. Top yolks with cheese, a dab of sour cream, reserved bacon and a black olive. Serve right away.

Makes 6 large skins.

Golden Broccoli & Ham Quiche Skins

6 large potato skins, lightly crisped

1 tablespoon butter

1 small onion, minced

1 small clove garlic, crushed

1 cup perfectly steamed chopped broccoli, well drained

½ cup diced smoked ham

2 eggs

¾ cup half~and~half

1½ tablespoons flour

½ teaspoon prepared hot mustard

¼ teaspoon seasoned salt

Fresh black pepper

Dash cayenne

¾ cup shredded sharp cheddar cheese

Garnish {6 large cherry tomatoes, sliced.

Preheat oven to 375°. In a small skillet melt butter; sauté onion and garlic until tender. Add the broccoli and ham, and sauté for another minute or two. Remove from heat and cool.

In a blender or mixing bowl, beat eggs with half~and~half, flour, mustard and seasonings until smooth.

Mix the cheddar cheese into the sautéed vegetable mixture and deposit an equal amount amongst your skins. Care~fully pour on the beaten custard.

Bake about 35 minutes. Place a sliced cherry tomato atop each skin, then return them to the oven for another 5 minutes, or until skins are done.

Makes 6 large skins.

Crab & Mushroom Quiche Skins

My absolute favorite.

8 large potato skins, lightly crisped

1 tablespoon butter
2 scallions, minced
1 heaping cup sliced mushrooms
1 clove garlic, crushed
1¼ cups flaked cooked crab meat

2 eggs
½ cup half-and-half
½ cup cottage cheese
¼ cup grated Parmesan cheese
2 tablespoons flour
¼ teaspoon seasoned salt
1 tablespoon chopped parsley
Tabasco to taste
1 cup grated Jack cheese

Optional Garnish {sour cream *and* paprika

🐚 Preheat oven to 350.° In a small skillet melt butter and sauté scallions, mushrooms and garlic until tender. Mix in the crab and sauté lightly for a minute longer; set aside.

🐚 In a blender, beat eggs with half-and-half, cottage cheese, Parmesan, flour, seasoned salt, parsley and Tabasco until well mixed. Pour into a bowl, and stir in the Jack cheese and the sautéed vegetable~crab mixture.

🐚 Place the skins on a shallow baking sheet. Fill each to the rim with an ample amount of crab filling. Bake for about 40 minutes, or until puffed and lightly golden.

🐚 Let skins stand a minute or two before serving. If desired, garnish each skin with a small spoonful of sour cream and dust lightly with paprika.

Makes 8 large skins.

Quiche Lorraine Skins

8 large potato skins, lightly crisped

10 to 12 slices bacon

2 cups grated Swiss cheese

4 eggs, beaten

2 cups half-and-half

¼ cup flour

½ teaspoon salt

Dash nutmeg

Dash cayenne

Garnish { paprika { crumbled bacon

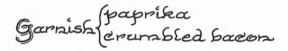 Preheat oven to 350.° Cook bacon until crisp; drain and crumble. Reserve some crumbled bacon for garnishing in the final step.

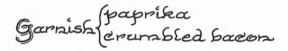 In each potato skin, sprinkle equal amounts of cheese. Top with crumbled bacon. In a mixing bowl, whisk together eggs, half-and-half, flour, salt and seasonings; _carefully_ pour over cheese.

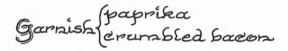 Bake about 20 minutes, or until firm. Cool a minute or two before serving. Decorate tops with paprika and re~ served bacon.

Makes 8 large skins.

Sweet Corn Custard Skins

Better make a lot of these — they disappear fast.

12 to 14 large potato skins, lightly crisped

4 cups corn, fresh or frozen
2 cups half-and-half
¼ to ⅓ cup sugar
½ teaspoon salt
2 tablespoons butter

4 eggs
½ cup finely snipped dates
⅓ cup slivered or chopped blanched almonds, lightly toasted
⅛ teaspoon cinnamon
4 slices bacon, crisply cooked and crumbled

Topping & Garnish { plain or honey-sweetened yogurt
cinnamon
extra snipped dates

Preheat oven to 325°. In a large saucepan, combine corn, half-and-half, sugar and salt. Simmer over medium-low heat, stirring frequently, until corn is tender, about 5 to 7 minutes. (Do not boil this.) Remove from heat, cool slightly, then coarsely grind corn mixture in a blender or food processor until it becomes a thick, chunky mass. (Do not purée.) Blend in the butter.

In a large bowl, beat eggs until frothy. Add corn mixture, along with dates, almonds, cinnamon and bacon — mix well.

Place the skins on a large baking tray. Spoon the filling to the top of each potato skin, stirring the corn mixture in the bowl as you go to distribute the solids evenly.

Bake for 35 minutes, or until filling is firm and a knife inserted in center comes out clean. Serve hot, topping each skin with a dollop of yogurt, a sprinkling of cinnamon, and some dates.

Makes 12 to 14 large skins.

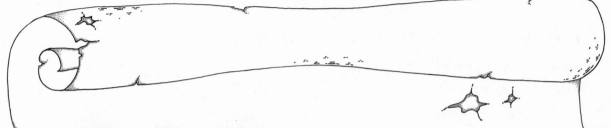

Beef, Pork and Ham Skins

Meat~and~potato~lovers unite! These skins are the ultimate combination of both. Just listen... tender beef strips in a sherry~spiked sour cream sauce... chunky chili topped with melted cheddar... pork and sauerkraut in a robust gravy... all filling up a crispy potato shell and served piping hot. One taste of a beef, pork or ham skin, and the meat~and~potato~lover in your house is destined to become a meat~and~potato~ SKIN~worshipper. It's just a matter of time.

Chili 'n Cheese Skins

10 large potato skins, crisped or fried and hot

1 to 2 tablespoons oil
1 lb. ground beef
1 cup chopped onions
1 cup chopped green bell
   peppers
1 large clove garlic, minced
1 15-oz. can tomato sauce
2 medium-size tomatoes,
   chopped
1 tablespoon chili powder

2 teaspoons brown sugar or
   honey
1½ teaspoons salt
¾ teaspoon cumin
½ teaspoon oregano
Fresh black pepper
1 bay leaf
Tabasco to taste
⅔ cup sliced black olives
1 16-oz. can kidney beans,
   drained

Topping { 2 cups grated cheddar or Jack cheese

Garnish { corn chips
         { diced onion

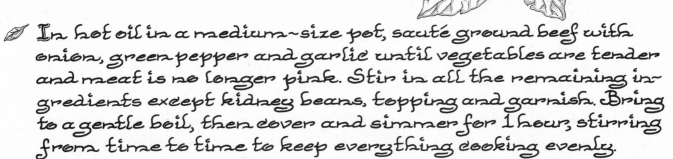

- In hot oil in a medium-size pot, sauté ground beef with onion, green pepper and garlic until vegetables are tender and meat is no longer pink. Stir in all the remaining ingredients except kidney beans, topping and garnish. Bring to a gentle boil, then cover and simmer for 1 hour, stirring from time to time to keep everything cooking evenly.

- Uncover pot, and stir in the drained beans. Heat a few minutes longer, or until chili is as thick as you like.

- Spoon the chili into your already hot skins, and top each generously with some cheese. Place under the broiler just until cheese is melted.

- Serve them hot, topped with corn chips and onion, or pass bowls of chips and onion for individual sprinkling.

Makes 10 large skins.

Mushroom Meat Loaf Skins

A remarkable dish.

10 large potato skins *

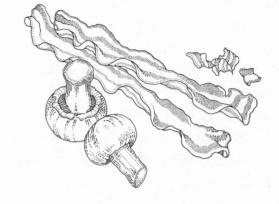

4 slices bacon, diced
1 cup minced onions
1 cup chopped mushrooms
1 large clove garlic, crushed
1½ lbs. extra lean ground beef
1 cup dry bread crumbs
1 cup half-and-half
1 egg, beaten
¼ cup <u>each</u> grated Parmesan cheese and chopped parsley
2 tablespoons catsup
1 teaspoon seasoned salt
Fresh black pepper
½ teaspoon thyme
Dash of nutmeg

Creamy Mushroom Sauce ~ recipe follows

Garnish {fresh chopped parsley

- Preheat oven to 350°. In a small skillet, sauté bacon until very crisp. Remove with a slotted spoon to drain, and crumble into tiny bits. Reserve all the drippings. In 2 tablespoons of the drippings in the same skillet, sauté onions, mushrooms and garlic until tender.

- In a large bowl, combine ground beef with all the remaining ingredients except Creamy Mushroom Sauce and parsley garnish. Be sure to include the sautéed veggies and cooked bacon. Mix together well.

- Pack each skin with the meat loaf mixture, sealing to the edges and building them up to rounded tops. Place the filled skins on a baking dish or tray, and proceed to bake them for approximately 40 minutes.

- Meanwhile, make Creamy Mushroom Sauce; keep warm.
- Place the hot baked skins on a large serving platter. Top each with an adequate helping of Creamy Mushroom Sauce, letting it run down the sides. Sprinkle with chopped parsley to serve.

Makes 10 large skins.

Creamy Mushroom Sauce:

Reserved bacon drippings plus butter to equal ¼ cup
2 cups thinly sliced mushrooms
¼ cup flour
1½ cups beef stock, heated
¼ cup sour cream, room temperature
Seasoned salt and fresh black pepper to taste
Pinch each of thyme and nutmeg
1 teaspoon dry sherry

- In a medium-size saucepan in drippings and butter (¼ cup total), sauté mushrooms until limp. Remove from heat and stir in the flour. Gradually add the stock, stirring until smooth and lump free.
- Return pan to medium heat and bring to a gentle boil, stirring constantly. Boil and stir 1 to 2 minutes longer.
- Blend some of the hot sauce into the sour cream. Return this mixture to the saucepan, mixing it all together well until smooth and uniform. Now taste. Add salt and pepper, thyme, nutmeg and sherry. Taste again to see if you approve. Cover and keep warm. (Do not boil this, but reheat gently before serving.

*Note: It is best to use skins that have a nice layer of potato left on them to soak up the flavor of the filling. Do not crisp or fry them first. Keep them dry instead. You can dry them out in your oven as you preheat it if you like.

Latin Meat Loaf Skins

6 large potato skins *

1 lb. extra lean ground beef

1 egg, beaten

½ cup dry bread crumbs

½ cup tomato sauce

¼ cup packed shredded cheddar cheese

¼ cup chopped or sliced olives (black or pimento-stuffed)

2 tablespoons diced canned green chilies

1 small onion, finely minced

1 clove garlic, finely minced

2 tablespoons chopped parsley

1 tablespoon vinegar

1 teaspoon salt

¼ teaspoon cumin

Fresh black pepper

Topping { ½ cup packed shredded cheddar cheese

Garnish { your favorite chunky salsa — mild to hot
{ sour cream
{ 6 whole olives — pitted, of course

◎ Preheat oven to 350°. In a bowl, gently combine all ingredients (except topping and garnish) until thoroughly mixed.

◎ Stuff the skins generously with the meatloaf mixture, spreading to the sides and making the tops full and round.

◎ Bake about 30 to 40 minutes, or until filling is firm. Top the skins with ½ cup cheddar the last minute or 2 of baking time.

◎ Garnish each skin with salsa, sour cream, and a whole olive.

Makes 6 large skins.

*Do not crisp or fry the skins first. Be sure they have a thin shell of innards still left on them for absorbing the meaty juices of the filling.

Swedish Meatball Skins in Dilled Mushroom Gravy

6 large potato skins, crisped or fried and hot

1 lb. ground beef
1 egg, slightly beaten
½ cup dry bread crumbs
⅓ cup half-and-half
¼ cup minced onion
1 tablespoon chopped parsley
1 teaspoon seasoned salt
⅛ teaspoon nutmeg
Fresh black pepper
Dash of dill weed

Garnish { chopped parsley

1 tablespoon oil
1 heaping cup sliced mushrooms
2 tablespoons flour
¾ cup beef stock
1 cup sour cream, room temperature
½ to 1 teaspoon dill weed
½ teaspoon seasoned salt
1 teaspoon dry sherry
½ cup freshly steamed peas

○ In a medium-size bowl, combine beef with egg, crumbs, half-and-half, onion, 1 tablespoon parsley, 1 teaspoon seasoned salt, nutmeg, pepper and a dash of dill weed. Shape into 1-inch balls.

○ Heat oil in a skillet and fry the meatballs gently, turning to brown all sides. Remove and keep warm, reserving the drippings.

○ In hot drippings, sauté mushrooms until tender. Remove from heat and stir in the flour, then gradually blend in the stock. Return to low heat and cook until thick and bubbly, still stirring.

○ Remove from heat once again, and blend in the sour cream, dill weed (start with ½ teaspoon and add more if you like), ½ teaspoon seasoned salt and the sherry. Heat very gently, stirring. Now, fold in the cooked meatballs and steamed peas, stirring carefully until all is thoroughly hot (but not boiling).

○ Spoon the meatballs into the skins and top each with some of the remaining gravy to cover nicely. Sprinkle with the chopped parsley.

Makes 6 large skins.

Beef & Potato Curry Skins

Don't let the long list of ingredients fool you. This dish is easy to make, very economical, and simply delicious.

6 to 8 large potato skins, crisped or fried and _hot_

½ lb. lean ground beef
1 onion, chopped
1 large potato, unpeeled and diced
1 small clove garlic, crushed
1 teaspoon grated fresh ginger
½ green bell pepper, chopped
½ sweet red pepper, chopped
¼ cup shredded coconut
1 tablespoon oil
1¼ cups water

2 tablespoons tomato paste
½ teaspoon _each_ curry powder and chili powder
¼ teaspoon _each_ cinnamon and turmeric
1 teaspoon salt
Dash of cayenne (more if you like your curry hot!)
1 to 2 teaspoons honey
¼ cup _each_ slivered almonds and raisins

Garnish { ½ cup plain yogurt
          ¼ cup lightly toasted coconut

FRESH-GINGER

In a medium~size skillet, sauté the first 8 ingredients in 1 tablespoon oil until beef is brown. Stir in remaining ingredients except garnish. Bring mixture to a boil, then simmer gently, uncovered, for about 20 minutes, or until thick and vegetables are tender. Stir frequently to keep it all cooking evenly.

Pile meat mixture generously into the skins. Top each with a spoonful of yogurt and an ample sprinkling of toasted coconut. Eat right away!

Makes 6 to 8 large skins.

Note: For an _almost_ authentic Indian meal, serve with chutney and a spicy lentil soup. Wonderfully filling.

Beef Stroganoff Skins

8 to 10 large potato skins, crisped or fried and hot

1½ lbs. sirloin steak
2 to 3 tablespoons butter
1 onion, chopped
1 clove garlic, minced
½ lb. mushrooms, thinly
    sliced
1 cup beef stock

2 tablespoons catsup
1 teaspoon salt
Fresh black pepper
3 tablespoons flour
¼ cup dry white wine
1 cup sour cream
¼ teaspoon dill weed

Topping
{
¼ cup each dry bread crumbs and Parmesan
    cheese
2 tablespoons melted butter
1 tablespoon chopped parsley
}

Cut steak into thin narrow strips; set aside. In a large skillet in hot butter, sauté onion, garlic and mushrooms until tender. Remove veggies from skillet, leaving the drippings.

Sauté beef strips in the same skillet until no longer pink. Add the stock, catsup, salt and pepper. Cover and simmer 15 to 20 minutes, or until meat is tender. (Test a strip of meat for tenderness.)

Stir the sautéed vegetables back into the skillet. Make a paste with the flour and wine, and blend this into the simmering meat mixture until thick. Add the sour cream and dill weed, stirring over gentle heat until everything is nice and hot — do not boil.

Fill the skins with the stroganoff. Toss together all topping ingredients and sprinkle over the tops. Broil briefly, just until crumbs begin to brown.

Makes 8 to 10 large skins.

Beefy Tostada Skins

Two skins per person is a complete meal.

12 large potato skins, crisped or fried and hot

1 lb. lean ground beef
1 medium-size onion, chopped
1 clove garlic, crushed
1 15-oz. can tomato sauce
2 tablespoons diced canned
    green chili peppers

2 teaspoons chili powder
1 teaspoon each oregano and
    salt
½ teaspoon cumin
¼ cup sliced black olives (re-
    serve a few for garnishing)

Unbeatable Tostada Topping & Garnish
1 16-oz. can refried beans, heated
2 cups grated cheddar cheese
2 cups very finely shredded lettuce
2 tomatoes, cut into chunks
1 avocado, cut into small pieces
sour cream
paprika
reserved sliced olives
your favorite salsa (optional)

In a large skillet, sauté beef with onion and garlic until beef is brown; drain off all fat. Stir in tomato sauce, green chilies, chili powder, oregano, salt and cumin. Bring mixture to a boil, then simmer, uncovered 15 to 20 minutes, until thick and flavorful. Stir in olives. (This filling can be made ahead of time and refrigerated for even more flavor. Reheat before filling skins.)

Spoon some hot refried beans (about 2 rounded tablespoons) into each skin and top with a layer of meat mixture. Sprinkle on half of the cheese—it will melt nicely into the meat. Top each with some lettuce, then the remaining cheese.

Arrange tomatoes and avocado on top of the cheese. Spoon on a dab of sour cream, followed by a sprinkling of paprika and an olive slice. Serve right away, with salsa.

Makes 12 large skins.

Pepper Steak Skins

8 large potato skins, crisped or fried and hot

1½ lbs. sirloin steak, cut into thin strips

2 teaspoons paprika

2 tablespoons butter

1 heaping cup thickly sliced mushrooms

1 cup scallions, cut on diagonal into 1-inch pieces

1 green and 1 red bell pepper, cut into strips

2 cloves garlic, crushed

½ teaspoon grated fresh ginger

⅛ teaspoon crushed red pepper

1 cup beef stock

¼ cup water

2 tablespoons each cornstarch and soy sauce

1 teaspoon sugar

Garnish {toasted sesame seeds

- Sprinkle steak with paprika. Heat butter in a medium-size skillet and sauté steak strips until no longer pink. Add the mushrooms, scallions, peppers, garlic, ginger and crushed red pepper. Continue to sauté 1 or 2 minutes more, then pour in the stock. Cover and simmer about 15 minutes, or until beef is tender.

- Meanwhile, combine the water with cornstarch, soy sauce and sugar. Stir into meat mixture until thickened.

- Fill the skins with the meat mixture, and top each with a sprinkling of sesame seeds.

Makes 8 large skins.

Note: 2 medium-size tomatoes (each cut into 8 wedges) can be stirred in along with the cornstarch mixture.

Burgundy Beef Stew Skins

10 large potato skins, crisped or fried and hot

2 slices bacon, diced

1½ lbs. beef stew meat, cut into 1-inch cubes

½ cup each chopped onion and green bell pepper

1 clove garlic, crushed

1 8-oz. can tomatoes, undrained

1 cup beef stock

1 cup burgundy wine

1 tablespoon chopped parsley

1½ teaspoons each basil and salt

¼ teaspoon thyme

1 bay leaf

Fresh black pepper

10 tiny pearl onions, peeled and halved

4 carrots, sliced ½-inch thick

4 small red potatoes, cut into chunks

1 cup fresh or frozen peas

3 tablespoons flour mixed with ¼ cup cold water

Garnish { fresh chopped parsley

○ In a large pot or kettle, cook bacon with beef, chopped onion, green pepper and garlic until meat is brown. Add tomatoes, stock, wine, parsley and seasonings. Cover and simmer gently for 1 hour, stirring from time to time.

○ Add pearl onions, carrots and potatoes to stew. Cover and simmer about ½ hour longer, or until meat and vegeta~ bles are tender. Add peas the last 10 minutes of cooking time.

○ Stir flour/water mixture into stew. Cook and stir until a nice gravy forms.

○ Spoon stew generously into each hot potato skin. Sprin~ kle with chopped parsley and serve.

Makes 10 large skins.

98

All American Burger Skins

BASIC BURGER SKINS:

8 large potato skins *

2 lbs. very lean ground beef
¼ cup finely minced onion
1 teaspoon salt, seasoned or regular
Fresh black pepper

8 slices of your favorite cheese

Various Extras
- mustard
- mayonnaise
- pickle slices
- catsup
- shredded lettuce
- alfalfa sprouts
- thinly sliced red onion
- fresh tomato slices

- Preheat oven to 350°. Combine beef with remaining ingredients except the "Various Extras." Press an equal amount of meat mixture firmly into each skin, filling completely.
- Bake for 20 to 30 minutes, or until as done as you like. Place a cheese slice over each baked skin (cutting to fit), then bake or broil just until cheese melts nicely over the top.
- Serve plain, or with any (or all) of the Various Extras.

Makes 8 large skins.

Note: Depending on the meat chosen, baked skins may need to be drained of fat before serving.

* Do not crisp or fry the skins first.

continued...

BURGER SKIN VARIATIONS:

Bacon & Swiss

~ Add a dash or 2 of cayenne to the meat mixture. Partially cook 16 slices of bacon and wrap 2 strips around each filled, unbaked skin, securing them at the top with toothpicks. Bake as directed. Remove picks. Top each skin with 1 or 2 thin tomato slices and a slice of Swiss cheese. Broil or bake until melted. Dust with paprika.

Pickle & Mustard

~ To the meat mixture, add 2 tablespoons of prepared mustard along with ¼ cup drained pickle relish. Bake. Top each with a slice of cheddar and broil or bake until melted. Garnish with pickle slices, catsup, and finely chopped onion.

Mushroom & Onion

~ Add ½ teaspoon of finely minced garlic to the ground meat mixture along with 2 tablespoons Worcestershire sauce and ¼ cup toasted sunflower seeds. Bake as directed. Meanwhile, sauté 1 cup each thinly sliced onions and mushrooms in 1 tablespoon butter with a pinch of fresh garlic until tender. Season with salt and pepper. Top baked skins with grated mild white cheese, sautéed veggies and a generous application of grated Parmesan. Broil.

Zippy Horseradish

~ Mix 2 tablespoons of prepared horseradish into the meat mixture.

Avocado & Sprout

~ Add ¼ cup toasted sunflower seeds to the meat mixture. Bake until done. Broil on some Jack or Muenster cheese. Garnish each skin with a pile of alfalfa sprouts, fresh tomato and avocado slices, a dollop of mayonnaise and a whole pitted olive.

Mexican~Style

~ To meat mixture, add ½ cup finely chopped green bell pepper, 1 teaspoon chili powder, and a generous pinch of cumin. After baking, melt on cheddar cheese. Garnish with shredded lettuce, salsa, sour cream, and chopped olives. Serve with crunchy tortilla chips.

Hickory Barbecue

~ Omit cheese. The last couple of minutes of baking time, top each skin liberally with your favorite barbecue sauce. Continue to bake until the sauce is nice and hot. Garnish with corn chips and lots of chopped sweet onion. Serve on a bed of shredded lettuce accompanied by crispy onion rings.

Pizza

~ Add ¼ cup grated Parmesan or romano cheese, ½ teaspoon each basil and finely minced garlic, and a pinch or 2 of fennel seed to the meat mixture. After filling skins, sprinkle on more Parmesan and bake. Top each generously with pizza or spaghetti sauce, a slice of mozzarella, and some sliced black olives. Bake or broil until cheese melts and all is thoroughly hot.

Curried Sesame

~ Toss ¼ cup toasted sesame seeds, 1 teaspoon of curry powder, ½ teaspoon of minced garlic, and a handful of golden raisins (optional) into the meat mixture. Bake as directed. Use a mild white cheese, or omit the cheese altogether. Garnish with chutney, and serve atop shredded romaine lettuce along with a marinated garbanzo bean salad.

Carnita Skins

8 large potato skins, lightly crisped and hot
1½ lbs. boneless pork shoulder, cut into small cubes
2 cloves garlic, finely minced
Salt (seasoned or regular)
Fresh black pepper
1 16~oz. can refried beans or 1 recipe Spicy Pinto Dip,
    page 24
Red and Green Chili Sauce (recipes follow)

Toppings
&
Garnishes
{
sour cream
diced avocado
grated cheddar or Jack cheese
sliced black olives
}

♥ Preheat oven to 350°. Rub pork cubes with garlic. Sprinkle with salt and pepper and place in a shallow buttered bak~ing dish. Add about ½ inch water to dish. Cover lightly with foil, and bake for 1 hour. Uncover and bake for an~other 1 to 1½ hours, or until meat is very tender and brown, and water has evaporated.

♥ In a small saucepan, heat beans until hot. Fill each skin with about ¼ cup beans. Top with the cooked pork cubes. Spoon on some Red and Green Chili Sauce. Top each filled skin with sour cream, avocado, cheese and olives, or pass these separately for individual garnishing.

Makes 8 large skins.

Red Chili Sauce

2 medium~size tomatoes
1 small onion, chopped
1 small clove garlic, minced
1½ tablespoons chili powder
½ tablespoon oil
½ teaspoon salt/pinch of sugar

102

Green Chili Sauce

1 tomato
1 4-oz. can green chili peppers, rinsed and seeded
1 small onion, chopped
1 clove garlic, minced
2 tablespoons chopped cilantro
1 tablespoon oil
½ teaspoon salt
Fresh black pepper

♥ For each recipe, peel tomato(es). To do this, place them in a pot of rapidly boiling water for 1 minute. Rinse under cold water and drain well. Slip off skins and chop.

♥ Combine chopped peeled tomato(es) in a blender with all remaining ingredients. Blend until almost smooth. Place each sauce in its own container and refrigerate several hours for best flavor.

Each sauce yields about 1 cup.

Sweet & Sour Pork Skins

8 large potato skins, crisped or fried and hot
1 lb. boneless pork
1 egg, beaten
¼ cup each cornstarch, flour and cold water
½ teaspoon salt
Oil for deep-frying

1 tablespoon oil
2 scallions, sliced (reserve greens)
1 clove garlic, minced
1 large green bell pepper, cut into cubes
1 large carrot, thinly sliced on diagonal
1 8-oz. can pineapple chunks, drained (reserve juice)

1 cup chicken stock
¼ cup each vinegar and brown sugar
2 tablespoons soy sauce
2 tablespoons cornstarch
2 tablespoons cold water
½ cup sliced water chestnuts

Garnish { reserved scallion greens
         { toasted sesame seeds

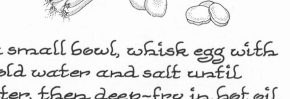

- Cut pork into ¾-inch cubes. In a small bowl, whisk egg with ¼ cup cornstarch, flour, ¼ cup cold water and salt until smooth. Dip pork cubes into batter, then deep-fry in hot oil (360°) about 5 minutes, or until golden. Drain on paper towels.

- In 1 tablespoon oil in a medium-size skillet, sauté scallions (whites), garlic, green pepper and carrot until crisp-tender. Combine pineapple juice with chicken stock, vinegar, brown sugar and soy sauce; blend into skillet mixture. Mix corn-starch and 2 tablespoons cold water. Add to skillet and cook and stir until thickened and bubbly.

- Mix in the pineapple chunks, water chestnuts and pork cubes. Stir gently until all is hot and well coated with the sauce.

- Pile some pork mixture into each hot skin. Sprinkle the tops with scallion greens and sesame seeds.

Makes 8 large skins.

Pork & Sauerkraut Goulash Skins

10 to 12 large potato skins, crisped or fried and hot

4 slices bacon, diced

2 lbs. boneless pork shoulder, cut into 1-inch cubes

2 onions, chopped

2 cloves garlic, crushed

3 cups beef stock

2 tablespoons paprika

1 teaspoon each caraway seed and salt

½ teaspoon dill weed

Fresh black pepper

2 16-oz. cans sauerkraut, drained

2 tablespoons flour

¼ cup cold water

1 cup sour cream

Garnish { crumbled cooked bacon
chopped parsley

In a heavy skillet, fry bacon until crisp. Drain well and crumble, reserving drippings. Sauté pork cubes in drippings until brown; remove with a slotted spoon. Sauté onion and garlic in remaining drippings until soft. Return pork to skillet along with stock, paprika, caraway, salt, dill weed and pepper. Bring to a gentle boil, then cover and simmer for 1 hour.

Add drained sauerkraut. Cover and simmer ½ hour longer, or until pork is tender. Mix flour and water and stir into skillet. Cook until mixture is slightly thickened. Over low heat, gradually blend in sour cream. Heat just until hot.

Heap a generous amount of goulash into each skin. Top with the crumbled bacon and chopped parsley.

Makes 10 to 12 large skins.

105

Sausage Pizza Skins

6 to 8 large potato skins, crisped or fried

¾ lb. Italian sweet sausage
1 medium-size onion, chopped
1 large clove garlic, minced
1 cup thinly sliced mushrooms
1 green bell pepper, chopped
1 8-oz. can tomato sauce
2 large ripe tomatoes, chopped
2 tablespoons chopped parsley

1 teaspoon basil
½ teaspoon oregano
¼ teaspoon salt
Fresh black pepper
Pinch of fennel seed
1 small bay leaf
1 teaspoon honey

Topping & Garnish {
2 cups shredded mozzarella cheese
¼ cup grated Parmesan cheese
½ cup sliced black olives

Brown sausage in a medium-size saucepan; crumble onto paper towels. Set aside ⅓ of the cooked sausage. In sausage drippings, sauté onion, garlic, mushrooms and green pepper until vegetables are soft. Stir in tomato sauce, chopped tomatoes, seasonings, honey, and ⅔ of the browned sausage. Bring mixture to a boil, then simmer, partially covered and stirring occasionally, for 15 minutes. (__Note:__ Now is the time to __preheat your oven to 400°__.) Uncover the sauce and cook for an additional 15 minutes, until thick and chunky, stirring every now and then.

Fill skins with sauce, then top each generously with mozzarella. Sprinkle on the reserved sausage, the Parmesan, and ultimately the olives.

Bake on a buttered tray for about 15 minutes, or until the skins are thoroughly heated and mozzarella is melted. Dig in!

Makes 6 to 8 large skins.

Western Hash & Egg Skins

Each crispy skin holds a savory ham hash, a baked egg, and a cheesy topping.

10 large potato skins, lightly crisped

3 cups cooked potatoes, cut into small cubes
2 cups diced ham
½ cup <u>each</u> finely chopped onion and green bell pepper
1 clove garlic, minced
1 teaspoon seasoned salt
Fresh black pepper
2 tablespoons butter

10 eggs
1¼ cups finely grated cheddar cheese

Topping { 2 medium~size tomatoes, each cut into 5 thin slices
{ grated Parmesan cheese

Garnish { chopped parsley

- Preheat oven to 350°. In a mixing bowl, toss together potatoes, ham, onion, green pepper, garlic, seasoned salt and black pepper to taste.

- Melt butter in a medium~size skillet. Gently sauté potato/ham mixture in butter about 10 minutes, or until golden.

- Fill each skin with the hot ham hash, leaving a slight hollow in the center. Carefully break an egg into each hollow. Sprinkle tops with cheddar.

- Bake about 20 minutes. Top each skin with a tomato slice and sprinkle with Parmesan. Bake for an additional 5 minutes — until eggs are perfectly set. Garnish with parsley.

Makes 10 large skins.

Scalloped Potatoes & Ham Skins

Quite impressive.

12 large potato skins, lightly crisped

1 lb. potatoes, pared and thinly sliced
1 cup diced cooked ham
3 tablespoons butter
2 scallions, whites thinly sliced; greens minced and reserved
3 tablespoons flour
2½ cups milk
½ teaspoon seasoned salt
Fresh black pepper
1 tablespoon diced pimento

Topping {1 cup shredded cheddar cheese, packed

Garnish {reserved scallion greens

- Preheat oven to 350°. Place potatoes and ham neatly into each skin. If potato slices are too large, cut them in half first.
- Make sauce: Melt butter in a medium-size saucepan. Add the scallion whites and sauté a minute or two. Remove from heat and blend in flour. Slowly stir in milk and seasonings.
- Bring sauce to boiling, stirring constantly over medium heat. Continue to boil and stir 1 or 2 minutes longer, or until thick and creamy. Fold in pimento. Pour sauce evenly over potatoes and ham in each skin.
- Cover with foil and bake 30 minutes. Uncover. Sprinkle tops with cheese and bake, uncovered, 45 minutes longer—or until top is golden-brown and potatoes are tender when pierced with a knife.
- Let skins sit 5 minutes. Sprinkle tops with reserved scallion greens and serve.

Makes 12 large skins.

Spicy Ham Loaf Skins

Don't be timid. Ask your butcher to grind the ham for you.

7 large potato skins, not crisped or fried

10 oz. ground cooked ham

10 oz. ground lean pork or pork sausage

2 eggs, beaten

1 cup fresh bread crumbs (leftover cornbread is nice)

¼ cup each minced onion, diced green pepper and chopped
   olives

¼ cup chili sauce

1 tablespoon chopped parsley or cilantro

2 teaspoons prepared mustard

1 clove garlic, crushed

Fresh black pepper

Topping {extra chili sauce or catsup

Garnish {chopped sweet onion
         {corn chips
         {sliced black or green olives

◎ Preheat oven to 350.° In a large bowl, combine all ingredi~
   ents except topping and garnish, mixing well. Press meat
   mixture into each skin, sealing edges.

◎ Bake about 1 hour, or until meat is done. Brush with
   extra chili sauce or catsup the last couple minutes of
   baking time.

◎ Serve skins hot, garnished as desired.

Makes 7 large skins.

Chicken, Fish and Seafood Skins

People are eating more chicken, fish and seafood now than ever before. They are good protein foods, but are lighter than beef or pork. They fill you up comfortably without giving you that "stuffed" feeling that often accompanies a meal of red meat. Imagine succulent boneless chicken mingling with freshly cooked vegetables, creamy sauces, and delicate cheeses... or shrimp with curry... crab and mushrooms... hot and cheesy tuna ...all floating on crispy potato boats, just waiting to be caught. Enjoy!

Cashew Chicken & Broccoli Skins

6 large potato skins, crisped or fried and hot

¼ cup oil — more as needed
1 cup whole cashews
2 cups uncooked chicken, cut into thin strips
2 cups packed broccoli flowerettes
4 large scallions, cut diagonally into 1-inch pieces (whites with some of greens)
1 carrot, thinly sliced on diagonal

1 clove garlic, finely minced
½ teaspoon grated fresh ginger
¼ teaspoon crushed red pepper
1 cup chicken stock
2 tablespoons each soy sauce and dry sherry
4 teaspoons cornstarch
2 teaspoons sugar
¼ teaspoon Chinese sesame oil
½ cup sliced water chestnuts

Garnish { toasted sesame seeds

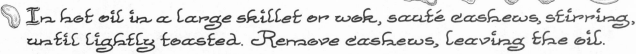

In hot oil in a large skillet or wok, sauté cashews, stirring, until lightly toasted. Remove cashews, leaving the oil.

Sauté chicken, broccoli, scallions, carrot, garlic, ginger and red pepper in remaining oil until veggies are crisp-tender and chicken is cooked (adding more oil as needed). Add the stock, then bring to a gentle boil.

Combine soy sauce, sherry, cornstarch and sugar in a small bowl. Add sesame oil and blend thoroughly. Add this to the simmering chicken and vegetable mixture, stirring constantly until the sauce thickens and boils. Mix in the toasted cashews and water chestnuts, stirring gently until all is hot.

Fill the skins with the sauté, mounting generously. Sprinkle the tops with sesame seeds. Serve hot, with extra soy sauce. (P.S. You may eat these with your hands if you feel the inclination to do so.)

Makes 6 large skins.

Chicken Enchilada Skins

Equally sensational made with turkey or cheddar cheese.

10 large potato skins, lightly crisped

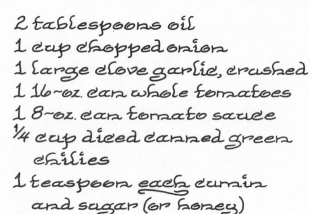

2 tablespoons oil
1 cup chopped onion
1 large clove garlic, crushed
1 16-oz. can whole tomatoes
1 8-oz. can tomato sauce
¼ cup diced canned green
   chilies
1 teaspoon each cumin
   and sugar (or honey)

½ teaspoon each salt, basil
   and oregano
¼ teaspoon coriander
Tabasco to taste
¾ cup sour cream
2 heaping cups coarsely
   chopped cooked chicken
2 cups grated Jack cheese
½ cup sliced black olives

Topping { 1 cup grated Jack cheese plus extra sliced olives

Garnish { freshly chopped cilantro or sliced scallions

In hot oil in a medium-size saucepan, sauté onion and garlic until tender. Stir in tomatoes (with liquid), tomato sauce, chilies, cumin, sugar, salt, basil, oregano, coriander and Tabasco. With a sharp knife or fork, break or mash tomatoes into small chunks. Bring sauce to a boil, cover, then simmer 20 minutes—stirring occasionally. Remove from heat and slowly blend in sour cream; set sauce aside.

Preheat oven to 350°. Butter 2 11x7x2-inch baking pans. Place 5 potato skins, side by side, in each pan. In a bowl, combine chicken with 2 cups cheese and ½ cup olives. Divide chicken mixture evenly into each skin. Pour ½ the sauce across the top of the skins in each pan and sprinkle each panful with ½ of the remaining cheese. Arrange a few olive slices over the top. Cover pans lightly with foil.

Bake about 40 minutes, or until thoroughly hot and cheese is melted. Garnish and enjoy right away.

Makes 10 large skins.

Curried Chicken & Mushroom Skins

10 large potato skins, crisped or fried

¼ cup butter
1 heaping cup chopped onion
1 clove garlic, crushed
1 heaping cup thickly
  sliced mushrooms
1 tablespoon curry powder
½ teaspoon salt
¼ cup flour
1 cup half-and-half

1 cup chicken stock
½ cup sour cream
1 tablespoon dry sherry
3 cups bite~size cooked
  chicken pieces
1 cup freshly steamed peas
2 tablespoons chopped parsley
A small handful of golden
  raisins (optional)

Topping & Garnish { more chopped parsley
½ cup lightly toasted cashew pieces

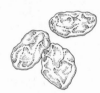

Preheat oven to 350°. Melt butter in a large saucepan; sauté onion, garlic and mushrooms until just~tender. Blend in curry powder and salt. Remove pan from heat, and stir in flour to make a smooth paste. Slowly blend in half~and~half, stirring constantly until mixture is smooth (except for the chunks of vegetables). Add chicken stock. Return pan to medium heat and bring to a boil, stirring. Continue cooking 1 to 2 minutes, or until thick and creamy.

Remove saucepan from heat and let sit a minute before blending in sour cream and sherry. Fold in chicken, peas and 2 tablespoons parsley. Combine gently, but thoroughly. (Toss in the optional raisins at this point, too.)

Fill skins with chicken mixture. Sprinkle tops with more chopped parsley and an adequate helping of cashews.

Bake skins until thoroughly hot — 10 to 15 minutes. Cover with foil while baking if you want them extra moist.

Makes 10 large skins.

Chicken Cordon Bleu Skins with Sour Cream Mustard Sauce

10 large potato skins, lightly crisped

10 thin slices cooked ham (about 8 oz.)
1 cup chopped cooked chicken
8 oz. Swiss cheese, cut into thin slices
1 large tomato, seeded and chopped
Seasoned salt and fresh black pepper to taste

Topping {
½ cup fine dry bread crumbs
¼ cup grated Parmesan cheese
2 tablespoons melted butter

Garnish {Sour Cream Mustard Sauce—recipe follows

- Preheat oven to 350.° Place skins in a shallow baking dish. Cover skins with ham, cutting to fit nicely. Sprinkle the chicken evenly over each skin, then top with Swiss cheese, also cutting the slices to fit as neatly as possible. Top cheese with chopped tomato and sprinkle lightly with seasoned salt and pepper.

- Toss together all topping ingredients and sprinkle over tomatoes. Cover baking dish securely with foil.

- Bake skins for 15 to 20 minutes, or until heated through and cheese is melted. If you desire a crispier crumb topping, broil the skins briefly (after baking) just until they start to brown.

- While the skins are baking, make Sour Cream Mustard Sauce. Spoon the sauce generously over each sizzling skin and serve.

Makes 10 large skins.

Sour Cream Mustard Sauce:

2 tablespoons each butter and flour
3/4 cup milk
1/4 teaspoon salt
Fresh black pepper
1/2 cup sour cream, room temperature
3 tablespoons prepared mustard
1 to 3 teaspoons prepared horseradish (to taste)

Melt butter in a small saucepan. Remove from heat and whisk in flour. Add the milk gradually, stirring until the sauce is smooth and lump free. Add salt and pepper.

Cook over low heat until thick and bubbly, whisking constantly. Blend in sour cream, mustard and horse~radish. Keep warm.

Chicken Almond Skins
in Sweet & Sour Sauce

10 large potato skins, crisped or fried and hot

¼ cup oil
1 clove garlic, crushed
½ teaspoon grated fresh ginger
¾ cup blanched almonds
    (whole, halved or chopped
4 scallions, sliced thinly on
    diagonal (reserve greens)
1 green bell pepper, cut into
    small cubes
1 cup sliced mushrooms
1 cup Chinese pea pods,
    halved crosswise

1 carrot, cut into matchsticks
1 8-oz. can pineapple chunks,
    halved (drain, reserving juice)
2 tablespoons soy sauce
¼ cup each vinegar and
    brown sugar, packed
2 tablespoons cornstarch
1 cup chicken stock
2 cups cooked chicken
    chunks or strips
A few drops Chinese sesame
    oil ~ optional

Garnish {lightly toasted sesame seeds

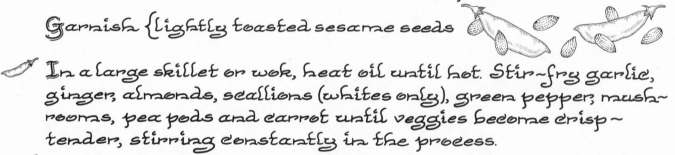

In a large skillet or wok, heat oil until hot. Stir~fry garlic, ginger, almonds, scallions (whites only), green pepper, mush~ rooms, pea pods and carrot until veggies become crisp~ tender, stirring constantly in the process.

Add pineapple juice, soy sauce, vinegar and brown sugar. Dissolve cornstarch in chicken stock, and add to simmering veggies, stirring until mixture is thick and translucent. Gently stir in chicken, pineapple chunks and scallion greens. Season with a few drops of Chinese sesame oil, if desired.

When chicken mixture is perfectly hot, spoon it into the skins, mounding it high. Scatter on some sesame seeds.

Makes 10 large skins.

Optional but LOVELY additions: Water chestnuts, thinly sliced; bamboo shoots; a handful of fresh bean sprouts; cubes of firm tofu.

Creamy Chicken Divan Skins

Steam the broccoli until just-tender and keep it covered.

12 large potato skins, crisped or fried and hot

¼ cup butter
2 scallions (whites only), minced
1 clove garlic, crushed
1 cup thinly sliced mushrooms
¼ cup flour
1½ cups chicken stock, heated

2 tablespoons dry sherry
⅛ teaspoon nutmeg
½ cup whipping cream,
   whipped to stiff peaks
½ cup freshly grated
   Parmesan cheese

4 cups hot cooked broccoli flowerettes
2 cups chopped cooked chicken (or turkey)
~Extra grated Parmesan~

Garnish { sour cream
          12 small whole mushrooms, sautéed in butter

In hot butter in a medium-size saucepan, sauté scallions, garlic and mushrooms until tender. Remove pan from heat, sprinkle in the flour, and stir to a paste. Slowly add the chicken stock until mixture is smooth.

Bring mixture to a gentle boil, stirring constantly with a wooden spoon. Boil and stir for another minute, until sauce has thickened. Remove pan from heat and mix in sherry and nutmeg. Carefully fold in whipped cream and ½ cup Par~mesan; set aside.

Fill skins with the hot broccoli and top with cooked chicken pieces. Generously spoon sauce over each skin, letting it run to the bottom. Sprinkle with extra Parmesan.

Broil until tops begin to brown and the sensuous aroma fills your entire kitchen. Garnish each skin with a dollop of sour cream and a sautéed whole mushroom.

Makes 12 large skins.

Chicken Skins Parmigiana

10 large potato skins, crisped or fried

2½ lbs. chicken breasts
   (skinned, boned, and cut
   into ¾ inch wide strips)
2 eggs, beaten
1 cup dry bread crumbs
1 teaspoon salt
Fresh black pepper
Oil for frying

1 tablespoon butter
1 small onion, diced
1 clove garlic, crushed
1 cup sliced mushrooms
2 8-oz. cans tomato sauce
1 large tomato, chopped
1 teaspoon sugar
¼ teaspoon each salt and basil

Topping { ¼ cup grated Parmesan cheese
1 heaping cup shredded mozzarella cheese
10 whole pitted black olives

Garnish { chopped parsley

🥫 Dip the chicken strips first into the beaten eggs, then into a combination of bread crumbs, 1 teaspoon salt and black pepper. Fry the chicken slowly in a ½-inch deep pool of hot oil until golden brown and tender. Drain well and keep warm.

🥫 Preheat oven to 350°. In a medium-size saucepan in 1 tablespoon butter, sauté onion, garlic and mushrooms until soft and tender. Add tomato sauce, chopped tomato, sugar, salt and basil. Bring to a gentle boil. Simmer, un-covered, for 15 to 20 minutes, stirring frequently.

🥫 Place about 3 cooked chicken strips (enough to fill) lengthwise into each skin. Pour on the tomato sauce, sprinkle each with some Parmesan, then pile on a gen-erous amount of mozzarella. Top each with an olive.

🥫 Bake, uncovered, for about 15 minutes, or until mozza-rella is melted and everything is sizzling hot. Garnish with chopped parsley.

Makes 10 large skins.

Chicken Liver Stroganoff Skins

6 large potato skins, crisped or fried and hot

6 slices lean bacon, diced

1 lb. chicken livers

2 heaping cups sliced mushrooms

1 onion, chopped

1 clove garlic, crushed

½ cup fresh or frozen peas

2 tablespoons flour

½ cup beef stock

1 tablespoon catsup

½ teaspoon each seasoned salt and Worcestershire sauce

Fresh black pepper

⅛ teaspoon dill weed

½ cup sour cream

1 teaspoon dry sherry

Topping & Garnish { dollops of sour cream / chopped fresh parsley

♪ In a large skillet, sauté bacon slightly, then add the livers and cook until brown on all sides. Remove bacon and livers and set aside, leaving drippings in skillet.

♪ In drippings, sauté mushrooms, onion, garlic and peas until tender. Combine the flour, stock and catsup in a small bowl, stirring until smooth. Add to skillet mixture, stirring until thick. Return liver and bacon to skillet, along with seasoned salt, Worcestershire, pepper and dill weed. Stir until nice and hot.

♪ Over low heat, gradually blend in sour cream and sherry until thick and creamy. Heat very gently without boiling.

♪ Fill skins. Spoon a small dollop of sour cream in the center of each, and sprinkle on some fresh parsley.

Makes 6 large skins

119

Chicken Taco Skins with Crispy Tortilla Strips

6 large potato skins, crisped or fried and hot

1 tablespoon oil
1 small onion, chopped
¼ cup diced green bell pepper
1 small clove garlic, crushed
1 8-oz. can tomato sauce
¼ teaspoon each salt, cumin, and crushed red pepper
Pinch of sugar
2 cups chopped cooked chicken

½ cup grated Jack or cheddar cheese
1 heaping cup finely shredded lettuce
Crispy Tortilla Strips — recipe follows
½ cup each Chunky Guacamole Dip (page 23) and sour cream
6 whole pitted olives

∨ In oil in a medium-size saucepan or skillet, sauté onion, bell pepper and garlic until soft. Blend in tomato sauce and seasonings. Cover and simmer 5 to 10 minutes. Mix in chicken and cook over low heat (uncovered) until hot, stirring often.

∨ Fill skins with the hot chicken mixture. Immediately top with grated cheese, then a helping of lettuce. Sprinkle on some Crispy Tortilla Strips, followed by spoonfuls of Chunky Guacamole Dip and sour cream. Finally, position an olive in the center of each skin and serve.

Makes 6 large skins.

Crispy Tortilla Strips:

2 corn tortillas   Halve tortillas, then cut the halves
Oil for frying   into thin strips. Sauté the strips in
Salt   a shallow pool of hot oil until crispy.
                          Drain well and sprinkle with salt.

120

Chicken à la King Skins

Chicken and fresh vegetables in a creamy herb sauce under a buttery crouton topping.

12 large potato skins, crisped or fried

½ cup butter
1 medium-size onion, chopped
A generous ½ cup each: thinly sliced mushrooms, celery, carrots and peas ← not sliced
½ cup flour
2 cups half-and-half

1¾ cups chicken stock
1 teaspoon seasoned salt
¼ teaspoon each black pepper and thyme
1 tablespoon minced parsley
3 cups cubed cooked chicken

Topping { 1 heaping cup of your favorite croutons
2 tablespoons melted butter
pinch each of seasoned salt and thyme

Garnish { chopped parsley

➤ Preheat oven to 350.° In a large saucepan, melt ½ cup butter. Sauté onion, mushrooms, celery, carrots and peas over medium-low heat, stirring frequently until veggies are just-tender. (Cover the pan occasionally to steam them along.)

➤ Remove pan from heat and stir in flour. Gradually blend in half-and-half and stock until smooth. Bring to a boil over medium heat, stirring. Add seasoned salt, pepper, thyme and minced parsley. Stir constantly as the sauce boils for about 2 minutes, or until thick. Mix in chicken.

➤ Fill skins with chicken mixture. Combine all topping ingredients (you have permission to use your fingers, if need be) and evenly sprinkle over each skin.

➤ Bake skins for 15 to 20 minutes, or until heated through. Garnish each with some chopped parsley before serving.

Makes 12 large skins.

Crab, Artichoke & Egg Skins au Gratin

An ingenious way to extend crab meat.

6 large potato skins, crisped or fried and hot
3 tablespoons each butter and flour
1½ cups half-and-half (may use part milk)
½ teaspoon salt
Fresh black pepper
Cayenne to taste
½ cup packed grated Swiss cheese
1 tablespoon dry sherry (more to taste)
1 cup cooked and flaked crab meat
1½ cups cooked artichoke hearts, cut into fork-size chunks
2 hard-cooked eggs, cut up

Topping {½ cup grated Swiss cheese
{3 to 4 tablespoons grated Parmesan cheese

Garnish {paprika

Melt butter in a medium-size saucepan. Whisk in the flour until smooth and bubbly. Slowly blend in half-and-half and seasonings and bring mixture to a boil, whisking constantly. Boil 1 to 2 minutes longer. Mix in ½ cup Swiss cheese and the sherry. Fold in crab, artichoke hearts and eggs. Cook gently over low heat, until everything is hot.

Place the skins on a broiler tray and fill them with the crab mixture. Top with the remaining ½ cup of Swiss and a generous application of Parmesan.

Broil until the Swiss cheese melts nicely, and tops turn golden.

To serve, dust each skin lightly with paprika.

Makes 6 large skins.

122

French Scallop Skins

6 to 8 large potato skins, crisped or fried and hot

1½ lbs. scallops
1 tablespoon each butter
  and lemon juice
¾ teaspoon salt
Dash each of marjoram
  and paprika
¾ cup dry white wine
⅓ cup butter
1½ cups sliced mushrooms

2 scallions (whites thinly sliced,
  greens minced and reserved)
1 clove garlic, crushed
¼ cup flour
1 cup half-and-half
1 tablespoon chopped parsley
¼ cup packed grated Swiss
  cheese

Topping {½ cup dry French bread crumbs
        {1 tablespoon melted butter

Garnish {reserved scallion greens

If scallops are very large, cut them into 3 or 4 pieces. Melt 1 tablespoon butter in a small skillet. Sauté scallops for 1 minute, then add lemon juice, marjoram, paprika and wine. Simmer gently, uncovered, 10 minutes. Drain scallops, reserving liquid.

Meanwhile, melt ⅓ cup butter in a medium-size saucepan. Sauté mushrooms, scallion whites and garlic until tender. Remove pan from heat and stir in flour. Slowly blend in half-and-half and reserved liquid. Bring to a boil, stirring constantly. Boil and stir 1 to 2 minutes longer, or until thick and creamy.

Over low heat, blend in parsley, Swiss cheese and scallops. Fill skins with scallop mixture. Toss together bread crumbs and 1 tablespoon melted butter. Sprinkle over tops.

Broil until crumbs turn golden brown. Sprinkle with reserved scallion greens and serve.

Makes 6 to 8 large skins.

Shrimp & Pepper Curry Skins

A creamy, chunky curry.

12 large potato skins, crisped or fried and hot

6 tablespoons butter
1 medium~size onion, cut
    into thin wedges
1 cup *each* thinly sliced red
    and green bell peppers
1 cup mushrooms, quartered
1 cup green peas, fresh or
    frozen
2 cloves garlic, finely
    minced

Pinch of crushed red pepper
    (very potent stuff)
1½ teaspoons curry powder
1 teaspoon salt
¼ teaspoon ground ginger
6 tablespoons flour
2½ cups half~and~half
½ cup sour cream
2 or 3 teaspoons lemon juice
2 cups medium~size cooked
    shrimp

Topping & Garnish { a dab of yogurt
your favorite chutney
lightly toasted whole cashews

Melt butter in a large saucepan or skillet. Sauté onion, red and green peppers, mushrooms, peas and garlic until veg~gies soften. Add crushed pepper, curry, salt and ginger. Continue to sauté until peas turn bright green and per~fectly tender. Remove pan from heat.

Gently stir in the flour. Slowly stir in half~and~half until smooth. Return saucepan to medium heat and bring to a boil, stirring constantly. Boil and stir 1 minute longer. Over very low heat, blend in sour cream, lemon juice and shrimp. Heat gently until all is hot and creamy.

Fill skins with curry mixture, and top each with some yogurt, chutney and a sprinkling of cashews. Serve.

Wait for compliments.

Makes 12 large skins.

Escalloped Crab & Mushroom Skins

Luscious crab and mushrooms—the ultimate!

6 large potato skins, lightly crisped

¼ cup butter
1 small onion, diced
1 clove garlic, finely minced
1½ cups sliced mushrooms
¼ cup flour
1½ cups half-and-half
½ teaspoon salt

Dash each of black pepper and nutmeg
2 tablespoons each dry sherry and diced pimento
2 egg yolks, beaten
2 generous cups cooked and flaked crab meat

Topping {
¼ cup dry bread crumbs
¼ cup sliced or chopped lightly toasted almonds
1 tablespoon melted butter

Garnish {chopped fresh parsley

◈ Preheat oven to 350°. Melt butter in a medium-size saucepan and sauté onion, garlic and mushrooms until tender. Remove from heat and stir in flour. Blend in half-and-half, salt, pepper and nutmeg.

◈ Return saucepan to heat and bring to a boil, stirring constantly. Boil and stir 2 minutes, or until sauce is thick and smooth. Remove from heat and blend in sherry and pimento.

◈ Mix a little hot sauce into the egg yolks, then return this egg/sauce mixture back into the saucepan and stir over low heat until quite thick—a minute or 2. Fold in crab meat.

◈ Fill skins with crab/mushroom sauce. Toss together bread crumbs, almonds and melted butter. Sprinkle over the tops.

◈ Bake about 20 minutes, or until filling is deliciously hot and crumbs begin to brown. Garnish with parsley.

Makes 6 large skins.

Fish Skins Amandine

6 to 8 large potato skins, crisped or fried and hot

1 lb. fish fillets *

1 egg, beaten

2/3 cup fine dry bread crumbs

1 teaspoon seasoned salt

Fresh black pepper

½ cup butter

½ cup slivered almonds

2 tablespoons lemon juice

Garnish {3 or 4 thin lemon slices, halved
{fresh chopped parsley

🍃 Rinse fillets in cold water and pat dry with paper towels. Place the egg in a small bowl. Combine the crumbs, salt and pepper on a flat dinner plate. Dip the fillets into the beaten egg, then into bread crumb mixture, coating well.

🍃 Melt ¼ cup butter in a large skillet. Over medium heat, cook the fish on each side 5 minutes, or until golden brown and flaky. Lay the fillets on top of the hot skins (cutting to fit, if necessary) and keep warm.

🍃 Melt remaining ¼ cup butter in the same skillet. Add the almonds and sauté until golden. Remove from heat and stir in lemon juice.

🍃 Immediately pour the lemon~butter sauce and almonds evenly over each hot skin. Lay a halved lemon slice on top and sprinkle with parsley.

Makes 6 to 8 large skins.

* Sole, cod, snapper, etc. Thaw fish completely if frozen.

126

Lobster & Shrimp Newburg Skins

5 large potato skins, crisped or fried

2 tablespoons each butter and flour
1¼ cups half-and-half
¼ teaspoon salt (more to taste)
⅛ teaspoon paprika
Fresh black pepper
Dash of cayenne

3 egg yolks, beaten
¼ cup dry white wine
½ lb. combined cooked lobster and shrimp
⅓ cup freshly steamed green peas
2 tablespoons diced pimento

Topping {
1 heaping cup sliced mushrooms
1 tablespoon butter
seasoned salt
grated Parmesan cheese

Garnish { paprika

Preheat oven to 350.° In a medium~size saucepan, melt 2 tablespoons butter. Blend in flour. Gradually stir in half~and~half and seasonings until smooth. Cook over low heat until sauce thickens and boils for 1 minute. Whisk constantly.

Add a small amount of sauce to the beaten yolks. Return yolk mixture to saucepan and cook until thick and smooth, still stirring. Blend in wine, seafood, peas and pimento.

Fill potato skins with seafood mixture. In a small skillet, sauté mushrooms in 1 tablespoon butter with a sprinkling of seasoned salt until just~tender. Top filled skins with mushrooms and sprinkle with Parmesan.

Bake 15 minutes, or until heated through. Dust lightly with paprika before serving.

Makes 5 large skins.

Tuna, Spinach & Cheese Skins

6 to 8 large potato skins, lightly crisped

2 tablespoons butter

1 medium~size onion, finely minced

1 cup chopped mushrooms

1 12½~oz. can tuna, drained and flaked

1 10~oz. package frozen chopped spinach, thawed and
   squeezed dry

3 or 4 slices fresh bread, made into crumbs (about 1½ cups)

½ cup sour cream

2 eggs, slightly beaten

2 tablespoons fresh lemon juice

Salt and pepper to taste

Dash or 2 of Tabasco

½ cup finely grated cheddar cheese

Topping { 6 to 8 slices cheddar cheese

Garnish { dollops of sour cream
          paprika

Preheat oven to 350.° In hot butter in a small skillet, sauté onion and mushrooms until soft; set aside.

In a large bowl, combine tuna with spinach, bread crumbs, sour cream, eggs, lemon juice, seasonings, ½ cup grated cheddar and the sautéed onion mixture; blend well.

Pack tuna mixture into skins. Bake, uncovered, 30 min~utes. Lay a cheese slice neatly upon each skin and continue baking 10 minutes longer.

To serve, top each skin with a dollop of sour cream and a sprinkle of paprika.

Makes 6 to 8 large skins.

Note: Crumbled cooked bacon may be added to the tuna mixture, or sprinkled on later as a garnish.

128

Cauliflower & Crab Mornay Skins

Each forkful calls for another.

8 large potato skins, crisped or fried
6 tablespoons <u>each</u> butter and flour
1½ cups milk
1 cup half-and-half
1 teaspoon salt
2 cups freshly steamed cauliflower, broken into small
    pieces
2 cups flaked cooked crab meat
1 cup freshly steamed green peas
¾ cup packed shredded Swiss cheese

Topping & Garnish { 1 cup soft French bread crumbs
{ 2 tablespoons melted butter

Preheat oven to 350°. In a large saucepan, melt 6 tablespoons butter. Remove from heat and blend in flour. Slowly stir in milk and half-and-half until smooth. Add salt. Return pan to medium heat, stirring continuously until sauce thickens and boils for 1 minute.

Fold in cauliflower, crab and peas (all well drained, of course). Fill skins with crab mixture. Sprinkle each generously with cheese. Combine topping ingredients and sprinkle over each skin.

Bake, uncovered, 15 to 20 minutes. Serve piping hot.

Makes 8 large skins.

Vegetarian and Vegetable Skins

There's something about a vegetarian or vegetable meal that instantly turns off typical meat-eaters. Most of them are convinced that a meal without meat cannot be satisfying. Worst of all, many meat-and-potato-eaters think vegetarianism to be soybeans, brewer's yeast and alfalfa sprouts — period.

I grew up with an intense hatred for vegetables (just like I hated insects). To this day, I still despise insects, but somewhere along the line I was transformed into a genuine vegetable-lover. I started cooking with fresh vegetables (whenever possible), learned how to steam them, season them, and skillfully combine them in ways which enhance their delicate qualities.

Once you sample a non-meat creation heightened by the presence of a crispy potato shell, you will experience the best of both worlds — something light yet deliciously satisfying. Guaranteed, you won't even miss the meat. And if you're a vegetarian or enjoy meatless meals, this section will hopefully encourage you to serve many a non-meat specialty cradled by a crunchy potato skin.

P.S. Don't be afraid to offer these Vegetarian or Vegetable Skins as side dishes accompanying a plain meat, fish, or fowl entrée, too.

130

Refrito Burrito Skins

10 large potato skins, crisped or fried

2 cups raw pinto beans
¼ cup oil
¼ cup soy bacon bits
1½ cups chopped onions
1 cup finely diced green bell
   pepper

2 large cloves garlic, crushed
2 teaspoons cumin
1½ teaspoons seasoned salt
¼ teaspoon coriander
Mucho fresh black pepper
Dash Tabasco~ to taste

Topping {1½ cups lightly packed grated cheddar cheese
         {¼ cup sliced black olives

Garnish {sour cream
        {your favorite chunky salsa
        {1 large scallion, minced
        {10 tortilla chips

Wash the beans well. Cover with cold water and let them soak overnight in a large pot. Next day, bring beans to a boil, adding extra water to cover beans completely. Simmer, covered, about 1½ hours, or until beans are very soft. Drain and mash beans until they are a smooth mass. Cover and keep warm.

Preheat oven to 350.° Heat oil in a large skillet. Over low heat, cook bacon bits, onions, green pepper and garlic, partially covered for 5 minutes, stirring often. Stir in cumin, salt and coriander. Cook 3 more minutes, or until veggies are tender. Stir in the mashed beans, and season to taste with black pepper and Tabasco. Continue cooking 1 or 2 minutes longer to mingle flavors.

Stuff the potato skins, filling them rather generously. Sprinkle surfaces with cheese and top with olives.

Bake 10 to 15 minutes, or until hot and cheese melts nicely. To garnish: First a spoonful of sour cream in the center... followed by a dab of salsa...a sprinkling of scallion...and a crunchy tortilla chip to crown each loving creation.

Makes 10 large skins.

Falafel Skins with Cucumber & Yogurt Topping

10 large potato skins, crisped or fried and hot

4 cups cooked garbanzo beans, drained
2 tablespoons oil
2 large cloves garlic, crushed
½ cup each minced celery and scallions
1½ teaspoons seasoned salt
½ teaspoon each turmeric and cumin
¼ teaspoon cayenne
Fresh black pepper
2 eggs, beaten
¼ cup tahini (sesame seed paste)
Dash of soy sauce
¼ cup lightly toasted sunflower seeds

Topping { melted butter
          { sesame seeds

Garnish { Cucumber & Yogurt Topping ~ recipe follows
         { paprika

◉ In a large bowl, mash beans to a semismooth paste. (Do not purée!) Set aside.

◉ In a large skillet in hot oil, sauté garlic, celery and scallions until tender. Add mashed beans to skillet, along with salt, turmeric, cumin, cayenne and black pepper, blending well. Remove skillet from heat and mix in eggs, tahini, soy sauce and sunflower seeds.

◉ Stuff skins generously with bean mixture. Drizzle melted butter over the tops and sprinkle with sesame seeds.

◉ Broil (at close watch) until hot and surface is brown and crusty. To serve: Spoon a generous serving of Cucumber & Yogurt Topping onto each skin. Dust with paprika.

May also be garnished with chopped tomatoes and black olives.

Makes 10 large skins.

Cucumber & Yogurt Topping:

2 cups plain firm yogurt
1 6-inch cucumber — peeled, seeded, coarsely shredded
   and squeezed of excess moisture
½ cup minced red or green bell pepper
¼ cup minced scallion
½ teaspoon salt (or seasoned salt)
⅛ teaspoon cumin

 Combine all ingredients in a small bowl. Cover and chill.

Mushroom Ratatouille Skins

Two skins per person constitutes a healthy, filling main course.

12 to 14 large potato skins, crisped or fried and hot
¼ cup olive or salad oil
1 medium-size onion, chopped
2 cloves garlic, crushed
1 green bell pepper, diced
1 small handful of mushrooms, quartered
2 medium-size zucchini, cut into triangular wedges
1 small eggplant, cut into cubes
2 large, firm-ripe tomatoes, coarsely chopped
1 teaspoon each salt, basil and thyme
Fresh black pepper
¼ cup each chopped fresh parsley and sliced black olives

Optional Garnishes
{ a dab of sour cream
{ freshly grated Romano cheese
{ grated mild white cheese

actual size

- In hot oil in a large skillet, briefly sauté onion, garlic, green pepper, mushrooms, zucchini and eggplant until the veggies become hot and begin to steam.

- Stir in tomatoes, salt, basil, thyme and black pepper. Cover and simmer gently for 10 to 15 minutes, or until vegetables are just tender, stirring periodically. The last couple of minutes, mix in parsley and olives.

- Generously stuff skins with vegetable mixture, mounding them high. Top with one of the optional garnishes if you like, and serve hot. (If you're grating on a mild white cheese, stick the skins briefly under the broiler to melt.)

Makes 6 large skins.

Irish Potato & Cabbage Skins

5 large potato skins, lightly crisped

2 medium~size potatoes
2 tablespoons butter
¾ cup finely chopped onion
1 small clove garlic, crushed
2 cups packed finely shredded green cabbage
¼ teaspoon crushed caraway seeds
¾ cup cottage cheese
¼ cup sour cream
½ tablespoon lemon juice
1 teaspoon salt (regular or seasoned)
⅛ teaspoon dill weed
Fresh black pepper

Topping
&
Garnish { 5 slices Jack cheese
paprika

Preheat oven to 350.° Peel potatoes and cut into large chunks. Boil until very tender.

Meanwhile, in hot butter, sauté onion and garlic until veggies soften. Add the cabbage and caraway and cook until all is tender.

Drain the potatoes well, then mash them along with the cottage cheese and sour cream. Blend in the wilted cabbage mixture, lemon juice, salt, dill weed and pepper.

Generously fill each skin with potato mixture. Bake 35 to 40 minutes. Lay a slice of cheese on top of each skin and dust with paprika. Broil until cheese is melted and creamy.

Makes 5 large skins.

Savory Cornbread Stuffing Skins

8 large potato skins, lightly crisped

1 8-inch pan of cornbread, crumbled (about 8 cups)

½ cup butter

1½ cups diced celery

1 cup chopped onions

1 sweet red pepper, chopped

1 cup corn, fresh or frozen

¼ cup soy bacon bits

2 tablespoons <u>each</u> sunflower and sesame seeds

¼ cup chopped parsley

1 teaspoon salt

½ teaspoon <u>each</u> basil and thyme

Fresh black pepper

1 egg

½ cup milk

Topping {8 slices cheddar or Jack cheese

Garnish {paprika

Preheat oven to 325°. Place the crumbled cornbread in a large bowl and set aside. Melt butter in a heavy skillet. Sauté celery, onion, red pepper, corn, bacon bits and seeds until vegetables are soft. Add to the bowl of cornbread along with seasonings, mixing well. Blend in egg, then milk until all elements are moistened.

Pack a very generous amount of stuffing into each skin, making the tops high and round. Place skins in a baking dish and cover securely with foil.

Bake 30 minutes. Uncover, lay a cheese slice on top of each skin and bake 15 minutes longer. Sprinkle with paprika before serving.

Makes 8 large skins.

Broccoli 'n Cheese Skins

10 large potato skins, lightly crisped

2 tablespoons butter

½ cup minced onion

1 clove garlic, crushed

½ cup chopped mushrooms

1 lb. finely chopped broccoli, steamed just until tender
   and well drained

2 cups cooked brown rice

¼ cup sour cream

2 eggs, well beaten

1 cup packed finely grated cheddar cheese

2 tablespoons each chopped parsley and soy sauce

¼ teaspoon seasoned salt

Fresh black pepper

Dash of nutmeg

Topping &
Garnish
{ more grated cheddar
paprika
sunflower seeds

○ Preheat oven to 350.° In hot butter in a large skillet, sauté onion, garlic and mushrooms until tender. Mix in broc~coli and stir~fry a minute longer. Remove pan from heat and thoroughly mix in the rice. Blend in sour cream, eggs, 1 cup cheddar, parsley, soy sauce and seasonings. Combine gently but evenly.

○ Stuff the skins with broccoli mixture. Place them on a buttered baking sheet and top with more cheddar, a nice dusting of paprika and a few sunflower seeds.

○ Cover loosely with foil. Bake 20 to 25 minutes, uncovering skins the last 5 minutes.

○ Serve piping hot!

Makes 10 large skins.

Chili Con Queso Skins

Say cheese!

6 to 8 large potato skins, crisped or fried and hot
1 tablespoon butter
1 small onion, minced
1 clove garlic, minced (optional)
1 large tomato, seeded and chopped
1 4-oz. can diced green chilies
½ teaspoon salt
¼ teaspoon cumin
Fresh black pepper
½ lb. Jack cheese, cut into small cubes

Topping & Garnish
- dollops of sour cream
- pimento strips
- chopped cilantro or parsley

- Melt butter in a large skillet; sauté onion and garlic until tender. Stir in tomato, chilies, salt, cumin and black pepper. Simmer uncovered until nicely thickened, about 10 minutes or so.

- Over very low heat, stir in cheese cubes to melt. Continue to cook an additional 5 to 10 minutes, stirring every now and then.

- Spoon cheese mixture into potato cavities. Broil until cheese is bubbly and just starts to brown.

- Garnish skins with dollops of sour cream, pimento strips and chopped cilantro.

Makes 6 to 8 large (and zesty) skins.

Zucchini à la Parmesan Skins

Delicioso!

10 large potato skins, crisped or fried and hot
¼ cup oil (may use part olive oil)
3 or 4 cloves garlic, crushed
2 cups chopped onion
2 cups thinly sliced green bell peppers
1 cup sliced mushrooms
4 cups thinly sliced zucchini
1 large tomato, seeded and chopped
½ teaspoon each oregano, basil, fennel seed and salt
Fresh black pepper
½ cup each grated Parmesan and sliced black olives
¼ cup chopped parsley

Topping { 2 cups shredded mozzarella cheese
  &   { grated Parmesan
Garnish { 10 whole pitted black olives

- Heat oil in a heavy skillet. Sauté garlic, onion, green pepper, mushrooms and zucchini over medium heat, partially covered and stirring often, until tender — about 8 to 10 minutes.

- Mix in tomato and seasonings. Cook a minute longer, then stir in ½ cup Parmesan, the sliced olives and parsley. Mix together well.

- Stuff the skins with zucchini mixture. Sprinkle some mozzarella atop each skin, followed by a healthy dusting of Parmesan and a whole black olive.

- Broil until cheese melts and mixture starts to sizzle. Serve hot!

Makes 10 large skins.

Baked Apple & Potato Skins

Almost dessert!

10 large potato skins, lightly crisped

2 medium-size potatoes
⅓ to ½ cup half-and-half, warmed
3 tablespoons butter, softened
3 egg yolks
3 tablespoons honey
Salt to taste
2 medium-size apples, pared and coarsely grated
A generous handful of dark or golden raisins
¼ cup sliced almonds
3 egg whites, stiffly beaten

Topping {cinnamon
{extra sliced almonds

Garnish {sour cream or vanilla yogurt

Ⓞ Preheat oven to 350.° Boil potatoes until tender. Drain well and mash them in a large bowl. Slowly stir in the half-and-half, mixing until all is smooth. Beat in the butter, egg yolks, honey and salt. Stir in apples, raisins and ¼ cup sliced almonds. Gently fold in egg whites until uniformly incorporated.

Ⓞ Spoon filling into skins. Sprinkle tops with cinnamon and some extra sliced almonds.

Ⓞ Bake, uncovered, about 45 minutes, or until nicely browned and firm.

Ⓞ Top each skin with a spoonful of sour cream or yogurt. Serve right away.

Makes 10 large skins.

Nutty Avocado Skins

8 large potato skins, crisped or fried

2 medium-size ripe avocados (1 mashed, the other chopped)

2 tablespoons lemon juice

1 tablespoon oil — more as needed

4 scallions (whites chopped, greens minced and reserved)

1 clove garlic, crushed

2 tablespoons soy bacon bits

1 cup finely chopped cashews or almonds, lightly toasted

⅓ cup sour cream

½ cup each minced parsley and chopped black olives

2 tablespoons diced canned green chili peppers

¼ teaspoon seasoned salt

Fresh black pepper

Topping & Garnish { sour cream, paprika, minced scallion greens

- Preheat oven to 350°. Mix together mashed and chopped avocado with lemon juice; set aside.

- Heat oil in a heavy skillet. Sauté scallion whites, garlic and bacon bits until scallions are soft. Over low heat, gently blend in avocado mixture. Stir briefly, just to heat through. Mix in all remaining ingredients except topping and garnish. Continue to stir over low heat 1 or 2 minutes longer — until thick.

- Stuff the potato skins, mounding each one artfully. Bake 10 to 15 minutes, or until filling is hot.

- Garnish each skin with a dab of sour cream followed by a dusting of paprika and a few scallion greens.

Makes 8 large skins.

Chilies & Tofu Skins Rellenos

This dish is fashioned after a wonderful sandwich I ex~
perienced in a little cafe in Tiburon, California.

4 large potato skins, crisped or fried

2 tablespoons butter

1 lb. firm tofu, well drained and carefully sliced into 8
   pieces

Salt and pepper to taste

2 whole canned green chili peppers, halved lengthwise,
   rinsed and seeded

2 medium~size tomatoes, thinly sliced

4 slices Jack cheese

Garnishes ⎧ salsa
         ⎨ fresh cilantro sprigs
         ⎪ sliced black olives
         ⎩ thin avocado slices

◆ Preheat oven to 350°. In hot butter in a large skillet,
gently fry tofu slices over medium heat until lightly
crisp and golden brown on both sides. Season with salt
and pepper.

◆ Into each skin, place 2 slices of sautéed tofu. Lay half a
chili pepper on top, followed by 2 or 3 tomato slices.
Top each with a slice of Jack cheese.

◆ Bake 15 minutes, or until cheese has melted and everything is deliciously hot. Garnish as desired.

Makes 4 large skins, recipe easily doubled.

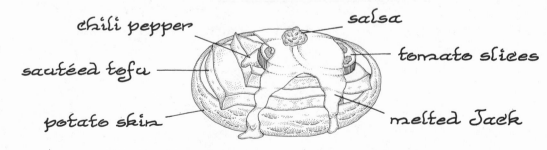

chili pepper   salsa

sautéed tofu   tomato slices

potato skin   melted Jack

Zucchini Kugel Skins

A light, yet filling supper dish.

6 large potato skins, lightly crisped

1½ lbs. zucchini, sliced
1 tablespoon butter
½ cup minced onion
1 small clove garlic, crushed
1 egg, slightly beaten

½ teaspoon seasoned salt
¼ teaspoon basil
Fresh black pepper
¾ cup shredded cheddar cheese (or Swiss or Jack)

Topping { ¼ cup fresh bread crumbs
1 tablespoon *each* grated Parmesan cheese and melted butter

Garnish { sour cream
paprika
fresh chopped tomato

○ Preheat oven to 350°. Steam zucchini until soft; drain well. With a mixer at low speed, break up zucchini into small bits. Drain again, pressing out most of the liquid. (Laying zucchini on paper towels helps to soak up excess moisture.)

○ Meanwhile, melt 1 tablespoon butter in a small skillet and sauté onion and garlic until tender. In a bowl, combine zucchini with onion mixture, egg, salt, basil, pepper and cheddar. Mix together gently but thoroughly.

○ Fill skins to the rim with zucchini mixture. Combine crumbs with Parmesan and melted butter and sprinkle over the tops.

○ Bake about 25 minutes, or until crumbs are light brown and filling is firm to the touch.

○ Garnish with sour cream, a dusting of paprika, and chopped tomato.

Makes 6 large skins.

Ricotta & Spinach Skins

Spinach~haters have been pleasantly surprised.

10 large potato skins, lightly crisped
¼ cup butter
2 scallions, minced
1 large clove garlic, crushed
¼ cup flour
2 cups half~and~half
½ teaspoon salt
Fresh black pepper
¼ cup grated Parmesan cheese
Dash of cayenne

2 lbs. fresh spinach leaves, steamed until wilted, drained,
   chopped, then pressed dry

2 eggs, beaten
½ cup ricotta cheese
1 cup grated Jack cheese
Squirt of fresh lemon juice
Pinch of nutmeg

Topping {extra grated Parmesan

Garnish {paprika
        {sliced black olives

🌿 Preheat oven to 375°. Make cream sauce: Melt butter in
a medium~size saucepan and sauté scallions and garlic
until tender. Remove from heat and blend in flour. Grad~
ually add half~and~half, salt and pepper, stirring until
sauce is smooth. Return mixture to medium~low heat,
and whisk constantly until it thickens and bubbles for
1 minute. Turn off heat, then stir in ¼ cup Parmesan
and cayenne to taste.

🌿 Remove ½ of the sauce, and mix it with the cooked and
well drained chopped spinach. Cover remaining sauce and

144

keep warm for the final step. Blend together eggs, ricotta and Jack cheese. Squirt in some fresh lemon juice and a pinch of nutmeg. Combine ricotta mixture with the "creamed spinach."

Fill skins with ricotta/spinach mixture and sprinkle tops generously with extra Parmesan. Bake 25 to 30 minutes, or until firm and tops begin to brown.

Stir remaining cream sauce in saucepan over low heat until hot—do not boil. Pour sauce over baked skins and sprinkle with paprika and olives. Serve immediately or place under broiler just briefly to brown.

Makes 10 large skins.

Fiesta Corn Skins

Works well with either fresh, frozen, or canned corn. But fresh is superior...as usual.

6 large potato skins, lightly crisped

2 tablespoons butter
1/4 cup each diced onion, green
   bell pepper and red pepper
1 small clove garlic, crushed
2 tablespoons soy bacon bits
2 tablespoons flour
3/4 cup milk
1/2 teaspoon seasoned salt

1/2 teaspoon paprika
1/4 teaspoon basil
Fresh black pepper
Dash of Tabasco
1/2 cup grated cheddar cheese
1 egg, lightly beaten
2 cups cooked corn

Topping {
1 tablespoon melted butter
1/3 cup coarsely crushed cracker crumbs
1 tablespoon sesame seeds

Garnish { fresh chopped parsley

- Preheat oven to 350.° Melt 2 tablespoons butter in a medi~um~size saucepan. Sauté onion, peppers, garlic and bacon bits until veggies are soft. Remove from heat and blend in flour. Gradually stir in milk.

- Return saucepan to heat and bring to a gentle boil as you stir in the seasoned salt, paprika, basil, pepper and Tabasco. Continue to boil and stir 1 minute longer, then remove from heat and blend in cheese, egg and corn.

- Stuff skins with corn mixture. Combine melted butter with crumbs; sprinkle atop skins. Top each with some sesame seeds.

- Bake 30 to 35 minutes, or until firm and lightly golden on top. Garnish with chopped fresh parsley.

Makes 6 large skins.

Creamy Sherried Mushroom Skins

8 large potato skins, crisped or fried and hot
1/4 cup butter
2 dozen large mushrooms, thinly sliced
2 healthy scallions (whites sliced, greens minced and
    reserved)
1/4 cup flour
1/2 teaspoon each seasoned salt, thyme and dill weed
Fresh black pepper
1/2 cup each dry sherry and sour cream

Topping { grated Parmesan cheese

Garnish { 8 parsley sprigs

🍄 Melt butter in a large skillet. Sauté mushrooms and scallion whites until soft and tender. Blend in the flour and seasonings.

🍄 Cook and stir gently over very low heat until quite thick—just a few minutes. Add sherry and stir until thick and creamy. Remove from heat and stir in sour cream and the reserved scallion greens.

🍄 Pile mushroom filling into the skins, mounding high. Sprinkle tops generously with Parmesan.

🍄 Broil until hot and Parmesan begins to brown. Garnish each succulent skin with a parsley sprig.

Makes 8 large skins.

Nut~Stuffed Skins

Dangerously nutty.

10 large potato skins, lightly crisped

3 tablespoons butter
1 large onion, finely chopped
1 large clove garlic, crushed
1¼ cups minced walnuts
1 cup cold cooked brown rice
¼ cup sunflower seeds
1 slice whole wheat bread,
   dried and crumbled
½ teaspoon seasoned salt

½ teaspoon thyme
Fresh black pepper
2 tablespoons soy sauce
¼ cup chopped parsley
1½ cups grated Jack or mild
   cheddar cheese
2 eggs, well beaten
⅓ cup dark or golden
   raisins

Topping   sour cream or yogurt
   &   paprika
Garnish   10 parsley sprigs

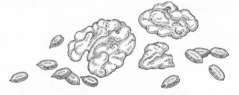

🥜 Preheat oven to 350.° Melt butter in a large skillet. Sauté onion and garlic until soft. Add walnuts, rice and seeds. Keep stirring over medium~low heat 5 minutes longer. Mix in the bread, seasonings, soy sauce and chopped parsley. Continue cooking another minute.

🌰 Remove skillet from heat and fold in cheese, eggs and raisins until evenly combined. Fill each skin completely.

🥜 Bake about 20 minutes, or until hot and filling is firm.

🌰 Spoon some sour cream on top of each skin followed by a light dusting of paprika and a fresh parsley sprig.

Makes 10 large skins.

Note: For a bit more greenery, toss in some steamed green peas or broccoli along with the cheese.

Spanish Zucchini Skins

6 large potato skins, crisped or fried and hot

2 tablespoons olive or salad oil

2 cloves garlic, crushed

1 cup minced onion

1 cup finely chopped green bell pepper

1½ cups (about) diced zucchini

½ teaspoon each seasoned salt, cumin, oregano and basil

Tabasco to taste

Fresh black pepper

2 tablespoons chopped canned green chili peppers

1 medium-size firm tomato, seeded and chopped

¼ cup sliced Spanish olives

1 cup packed grated sharp cheddar cheese

~Paprika~

Topping & Garnish { sour cream
Spanish olives, sliced or whole

◎ In hot oil in a large skillet, sauté garlic, onion, bell pepper and zucchini for a couple of minutes. Add seasonings and chili peppers.

◎ Cook over medium heat, uncovered and stirring often, until zucchini is tender but not mushy—about 10 minutes in all. The final 3 or 4 minutes of cooking, stir in the tomato and ¼ cup sliced olives.

◎ Remove skillet from heat and blend in cheese. Fill the skins generously with zucchini mixture. Sprinkle sur~ faces with paprika.

◎ Broil briefly, just until cheese starts to brown. Deco~ rate tops with sour cream and additional olives. Serve hot!

Makes 6 large skins.

Baked Broccoli &
Egg Skin Nests

You'll need 4 large, nicely rounded potato skins for this recipe.

4 large potato skins, lightly crisped
2½ cups coarsely chopped broccoli
Salt and pepper

1½ tablespoons butter
¼ cup minced onion
1½ tablespoons flour
1 cup half-and-half
¼ teaspoon each salt and dry mustard
Fresh black pepper
Dash or 2 of Tabasco
½ cup packed grated cheddar cheese

4 eggs

Topping
&
Garnish
{
2 tablespoons fresh bread crumbs
1 tablespoon grated Parmesan cheese
1 teaspoon melted butter

Steam broccoli until perfectly tender. Drain, if necessary. Season lightly to taste with salt and pepper; keep warm.

Preheat oven to 375° In a small saucepan, melt butter. Sauté onion in butter just until wilted. Sprinkle in flour as you stir, until mixture is thick. Remove from heat and slowly blend in half-and-half until smooth. Return saucepan to medium heat and bring to a boil, stirring continually. This is a good time, by the way, to season your sauce with the salt, dry mustard, pepper and Tabasco. Boil the sauce gently, stirring for a minute longer, then remove from heat and blend in ½ cup cheddar until melted.

To assemble: Place the freshly steamed broccoli in the skins, leaving a hollow space in the centers. Spoon sauce

150

over and around broccoli. Carefully break an egg into each hollow. Combine topping ingredients and sprinkle over your patiently awaiting eggs. (Do the above procedure with a light hand, taking care not to break yolks or have the whites run amok.)

Bake the "nests" for 12 to 15 minutes, or until eggs are set to your preference. Serve hot.

Makes 4 large skins; recipe easily doubled.

Optional Additions: a) ½ cup thinly sliced mushrooms sautéed with the onion.
b) 1 small clove crushed garlic, sautéed with the onion.
c) crumbled cooked bacon added to the completed sauce.

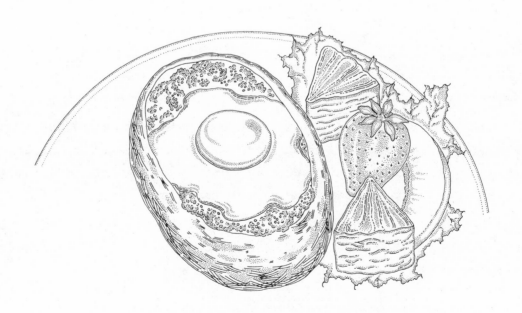

Cannelloni Stuffed Skins

Delightful for a small, intimate gathering. Recipe doubles or triples well, too.

6 to 8 large potato skins, lightly crisped
1 cup ricotta cheese
1 3-oz. package cream cheese, softened
2 tablespoons butter, softened
1 egg, beaten
1 scallion, finely minced
2 tablespoons chopped parsley
Salt and fresh black pepper to taste
A pinch of each basil and oregano
¼ cup grated Parmesan cheese

Topping { 1 cup marinara sauce (meatless Italian tomato sauce)
2 tablespoons grated Parmesan cheese

Garnish { chopped fresh parsley

- Preheat oven to 350°. In a medium-size bowl, mix together ricotta, cream cheese, butter, egg, scallion, parsley, salt, pepper, herbs and ¼ cup Parmesan. Combine well.

- Fill skins to the rim with cheese mixture. Place side by side (like filled enchiladas) in a flat buttered baking dish. Pour marinara sauce down center of skins. Sprinkle with remaining 2 tablespoons Parmesan.

- Bake, uncovered, for 25 to 30 minutes. Remove skins from oven, sprinkle with chopped parsley, and serve. Pass extra Parmesan to sprinkle on top.

Makes 6 to 8 large skins.

Apple, Raisin & Cheddar~Baked Skins

A bit like apple pie with cheese.

6 to 8 large potato skins, crisped or fried and hot

6 large apples, peeled and thinly sliced (about 6 cups)
2 tablespoons lemon juice
2 tablespoons butter
1 cup chopped onions
2 tablespoons honey
½ teaspoon cinnamon
A generous dash each of cloves and nutmeg

⅔ cup chopped lightly toasted nuts (recommendations: walnuts, pecans or almonds)
½ cup dark raisins
2 tablespoons apple cider vinegar
2 teaspoons flour
2 cups packed finely grated cheddar cheese

Topping
&
Garnish
(extra grated cheddar
(extra cinnamon
(extra chopped nuts

Toss apples with lemon juice. Heat butter in a large skillet. Cook apples and onions over medium heat, partially covered, until very tender—5 to 10 minutes. Stir mixture gently and frequently as it cooks. Mix in honey, spices, ⅔ cup nuts and raisins.

In a small bowl, stir together vinegar and flour. Add to apple mixture, stirring over low heat until slightly thickened. Blend in 2 cups cheddar, stirring just to melt cheese.

Stuff skins with apple mixture. Sprinkle tops with extra cheddar and dust with cinnamon. Toss on a few chopped nuts.

Broil until cheese is melted and creamy.

Makes 6 to 8 large skins.

153

Skinny Skins

Question: Can you indulge in the pleasures
of the potato and still be skinny?
Answer: Absolutely!

For years, people have been saying "no-no!"
to the poor potato for fear of gaining weight.
Actually, the GOBS of butter and sour cream
are the calorie culprits here—not the
potato. Here's a fairly accurate calorie count-
down. One healthy medium-size potato
weighing about ½ pound is approximately
145 calories. One whole skin is anywhere
from 25 to 50 calories, depending on the
size of the potato. So relax and enjoy. Just
go easy on the butter and sour cream!

The recipes in this section use an abundance of fresh vegetables, herbs, lowfat
cheeses, and other light stuffers that add
provocative flavor with a minimum of fat.
Most of them check in at under 200 calories. When you analyze this, you realize
that a lavishly stuffed skin has fewer
calories than a cup of sweetened yogurt.
So indulge without feeling guilty.

Light Cheeses

In order to keep the calorie count down, you will need to hold back on butter, sour cream and cheeses with a high fat content. There are lots of delicious naturally lowfat cheeses on the market that make excellent low calorie substitutes. You needn't resort to any of the synthetic varieties that are highly processed and contain many undesirable additives. (A friend of mine refers to them as "plastic cheeses"—and come to think of it, there is a close resemblance.) Here's a brief account of some lowfat cheeses that can be incorporated into the "skinny" potato experience with good results:

1~ <u>Farmers cheese</u>: A very dry cottage cheese. Crumble it into potato dishes, or use as a topping.

2~ <u>Feta cheese</u>: A snappy, salty cheese made from goats' milk. Often used as a topping in salads and casseroles.

3~ <u>Pot cheese</u>: Sold in "tubs" like cottage cheese, only firmer and richer in consistency.

4~ <u>Lowfat cottage cheese</u>: About 200 calories per cup. Contains less cream than the regular variety.

5~ <u>Hoop cheese</u>: Very high in protein. Use it in Buttermilk Sour Cream (recipe follows), or crumble it into or on top of just about anything.

6~ <u>Part~skim ricotta cheese</u>: A creamy, soft Italian cheese. Use it in desserts as well as hearty potato dishes, and ethnic favorites.

7~ <u>Part~skim mozzarella cheese</u>: Used in Italian cookery. Contains wonderful melting properties—makes almost anything taste like pizza!

8~ <u>Sapsago cheese</u>: A "green" cheese of Swiss origin. Very potent with a distinct flavor. Experiment with it, using it sparingly at first.

Buttermilk Sour Cream

Use this marvelous topping any time you crave REAL sour cream but will not succumb to its calories. Buttermilk Sour Cream is rich and thick and tastes exceedingly fattening—but it's not. It is very high in protein but modest in calories (just 15 per tablespoon), so you can afford to use it generously as a topping or in recipes calling for sour cream (dressings, dips, etc.)

1 cup crumbled hoop cheese
½ cup buttermilk, more if needed
1 teaspoon fresh lemon juice
Salt, plain or seasoned

Place ½ cup of the cheese, the buttermilk, and lemon juice in a blender or food processor. Process on high, until creamy and smooth. Add the remaining cheese, and blend again until quite thick—the consistency of sour cream. Season with salt to taste. Serve as is, or spice it up further with one or more of the suggestions which follow.

~ Fresh black pepper
~ Parmesan or Romano cheese
~ Soy bacon bits
~ Instant minced onion—lightly toasted
~ Garlic powder
~ Hot pepper sauce or Tabasco or your favorite salsa
~ Minced chives or scallions
~ Chopped or grated fresh veggies (carrots, cucumber, radishes, etc.)
~ Toasted sesame seeds
~ Herbs and spices: dill, parsley, mustard, curry, chili powder...
~ A little honey and cinnamon
~ Chopped ripe olives

Makes a generous ¾ cup, about 15 calories per tablespoon.

156

Steamed Fresh Vegetable Skins with <u>Melted Cheese</u>

The simplest of vegetable dishes.

8 large potato skins, crisped and <u>hot</u> using a minimum of butter

6 cups perfectly steamed and hot fresh vegetables*
Seasoned salt and fresh black pepper

Topping { 1 cup shredded cheese **
{ grated Parmesan

Garnish { paprika and/or chopped parsley

- Place a generous pile of hot, perfectly steamed veggies into each eagerly awaiting skin. Season lightly.
- Sprinkle each with 2 tablespoons shredded cheese, and dust the tops with Parmesan.
- Broil until cheese is nicely melted. Garnish with paprika and/or parsley to serve.

Makes 8 large skins, about 110 calories each, depending upon the choice of vegetables and cheese.

<u>*Some suggestions. Use one or more</u>: broccoli, tomatoes, carrots, cauliflower, eggplant, green beans, Brussel sprouts, mushrooms, onions, zucchini, other squashes.

** <u>Use just one, or combine them for many different results</u>: cheddar (mild to sharp), Muenster, mozzarella, Swiss, Jack, Gruyère, Fontina, etc.

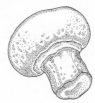

Creamy Chicken Skins in Mushroom, Pea & Onion Sauce

Rich and delicious.

7 or 8 large potato skins, crisped and hot using a minimum of butter

¼ cup flour
2 cups nonfat milk
¾ teaspoon salt
Fresh black pepper
1 cup grated Swiss or
   Jack cheese
1 tablespoon soy bacon bits

1½ teaspoons dry sherry
Dash of nutmeg
1 cup each freshly steamed
   sliced mushrooms, pearl
   onions, and green peas
2 cups cooked white meat
   chicken, cut into cubes

Topping
&
Garnish
{
2 tablespoons fresh bread crumbs
2 tablespoons grated Parmesan cheese
1 tablespoon chopped parsley

Place the flour in a medium-size saucepan. Slowly blend in the milk, salt and pepper until smooth. Cook over low heat, stirring constantly, until mixture thickens and boils. Boil and stir 1 minute longer. Over low heat, blend in the Swiss or Jack, bacon bits, sherry and nutmeg until smooth.

Add the steamed and well-drained vegetables to the sauce. Fold in the chicken, stirring gently until every-thing is nice and hot.

Fill skins with the chicken mixture. Combine all top-ping ingredients and sprinkle over the skins.

Broil just until crumbs start to brown. Serve.

Makes 7 (about 240 calories apiece) or 8 (about 200 apiece) large skins.

Chicken Mozzarella Skins

6 large potato skins, crisped and hot using a minimum of oil

1 tablespoon oil
1 cup chopped onions
2 cloves garlic, finely minced
1 heaping cup sliced mush-
    rooms
2 cups uncooked chicken,
    cut into chunks
1½ cups chopped fresh toma-
    toes

2 tablespoons tomato paste
2 tablespoons chopped
    parsley
½ teaspoon each salt and
    basil
¼ teaspoon thyme
Fresh black pepper
2 tablespoons grated
    Parmesan cheese

Topping { ½ cup grated mozzarella cheese, packed
         { extra Parmesan

Garnish { chopped parsley
        { 3 black olives, halved lengthwise

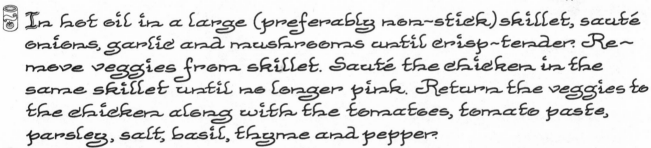

🥫 In hot oil in a large (preferably non-stick) skillet, sauté onions, garlic and mushrooms until crisp-tender. Remove veggies from skillet. Sauté the chicken in the same skillet until no longer pink. Return the veggies to the chicken along with the tomatoes, tomato paste, parsley, salt, basil, thyme and pepper.

🥫 Bring to a gentle simmer, then cover and cook 2 minutes, stirring twice. Uncover and continue to cook for an additional minute or 2, until chicken is tender and sauce has thickened slightly. Blend in 2 tablespoons Parmesan.

🥫 Spoon the hot chicken mixture into the skins. Sprinkle each with some mozzarella and dust lightly with extra Parmesan.

🥫 Broil at close watch, until mozzarella melts and tops turn golden brown. Garnish with parsley and olives.

Makes 6 large skins, each about 185 "delicioso" calories.

Eggplant & Mushroom Scallopini Skins

An Italian delicacy minus a lot of extra calories.

6 large potato skins, crisped and hot using a minimum of butter

1 tablespoon oil (olive or vegetable)
1 cup chopped onions
1 clove garlic, crushed
2 cups chopped mushrooms
4 cups eggplant, cut into ¾-inch cubes
2 medium-size tomatoes, chopped

½ cup dry white wine
2 tablespoons tomato paste
½ teaspoon each salt and basil
Fresh black pepper
¼ cup grated Parmesan cheese
2 tablespoons chopped parsley

Topping & Garnish { extra Parmesan, 6 parsley sprigs

In hot oil in a large skillet or saucepan, sauté onions and garlic until soft. Add mushrooms, eggplant and tomatoes. Continue to sauté for a couple of minutes longer.

Pour in the wine, tomato paste, salt, basil and pepper—mix together well. Bring to a gentle boil, then cover and simmer over low heat about 10 minutes, or until eggplant is tender. Stir mixture frequently.

Blend ¼ cup Parmesan and 2 tablespoons parsley into the simmering eggplant mixture until evenly combined.

Stuff each skin generously with the hot mixture. Top with a light dusting of Parmesan followed by a sprig of fresh parsley.

Makes 6 large skins, each containing about 120 calories.

Cottage Cheese & Zucchini Custard Skins

Absolutely delicious and low cal.

8 large potato skins, lightly crisped using a minimum
    of butter

1 cup packed shredded zucchini
1 lb. (2 cups) lowfat cottage cheese, drained
2 scallions, minced (whites with some greens)
3 eggs, well beaten
¼ cup grated Parmesan or Romano cheese
3 tablespoons flour
½ teaspoon each salt and basil
Fresh black pepper

Topping { 2 medium~size tomatoes, thinly sliced
          { extra Parmesan or Romano

Garnish { chopped fresh parsley

Preheat oven to 375.° Place zucchini in a strainer and
salt it lightly. (This will help draw out moisture.) Press
out the liquid and squeeze it dry on paper towels.

In a large bowl, whisk together cottage cheese, zucchini,
scallions, eggs, ¼ Parmesan, flour and seasonings.

Place the skins on a baking tray and fill them with the
cottage cheese mixture. Bake for 30 minutes. Remove
the tray from the oven and lay approximately 2 tomato
slices atop each skin. Dust lightly with Parmesan.
Bake 15 minutes longer.

Sprinkle with chopped parsley to serve.

    Makes 8 large skins, only 110 calories apiece.

Broccoli & Mushroom Quiche Skins

Each baked skin contains approximately 10 grams of protein.

10 large potato skins, lightly crisped using a minimum of butter

1 tablespoon oil
¼ cup finely chopped onion
1 small clove garlic, crushed
2 tablespoons soy bacon bits
2 cups finely chopped broccoli
1 heaping cup chopped mushrooms

1½ cups packed crumbled hoop cheese
1 cup nonfat milk
3 eggs
½ teaspoon salt
¼ teaspoon thyme
Fresh black pepper
Dash or 2 of nutmeg

Topping & Garnish {paprika

- Preheat oven to 375.° Heat oil in a medium~size skillet. Sauté onion, garlic, bacon bits, broccoli and mushrooms until veggies are crisp~tender. Set aside.

- In a blender, combine all remaining ingredients except paprika. Process until you have a smooth, creamy custard.

- Put the skins on a baking tray. Place an equal amount of vegetable mixture into each skin. Carefully pour the beaten custard mixture over the vegetables, filling to the rims. Sprinkle the tops with paprika.

- Bake about 40 minutes, or until firm and lightly golden.

Makes 10 large skins, each about 120 calories.

Ratatouille Quiche Skins

Quiche!

12 large potato skins, lightly crisped using a minimum
    of butter

1 tablespoon oil (olive or
    vegetable)
1 small clove garlic, minced
½ cup each chopped onion,
    green bell pepper and
    mushrooms
1 cup each diced zucchini
    and eggplant
1 medium~size tomato,
    chopped and drained (½ cup)

½ teaspoon basil
¼ teaspoon oregano
Salt and pepper to taste
4 eggs
1½ cups nonfat milk
3 tablespoons flour
¼ teaspoon salt
1 cup packed shredded
    Jack cheese
~Grated Parmesan~

Garnish (chopped fresh parsley and/or sliced black olives

Preheat oven to 375.° Heat oil in a medium~size non~
stick skillet. Sauté garlic, onion, green pepper, mush~
rooms, zucchini and eggplant over medium heat until
just~tender. Stir in tomato, basil, oregano, and season
to taste with salt and pepper. Remove from heat and
cool slightly.

Beat eggs well. Beat in milk, flour and ¼ teaspoon salt
until smooth.

Place an even amount of Jack cheese into each skin.
Top with the vegetable mixture, using a slotted spoon if
there is much liquid. Carefully pour the beaten custard
over all. Lightly sprinkle Parmesan over the tops.

Bake 35 to 40 minutes, or until set and golden brown.
Sprinkle with parsley and/or sliced olives.

Makes 12 large skins, each about 125 miniscule calories.

Cottage Scrambled Egg Skins

A fine, low calorie brunch selection.

8 large potato skins, crisped and hot using a minimum
   of butter

2 tablespoons butter
1 heaping cup chopped onions
1 heaping cup sliced mushrooms
12 eggs
1 teaspoon each seasoned salt and dill weed
Fresh black pepper
1 cup lowfat (or regular) cottage cheese
3 to 4 teaspoons soy bacon bits

Garnish { paprika
          { 12 parsley sprigs

- In a large, preferably non-stick skillet, melt the butter. Sauté onions and mushrooms until soft and tender.

- In a mixing bowl, beat eggs with seasoned salt, dill weed and pepper. Pour egg mixture into skillet. Cook for a minute or 2 over medium-low heat, gently folding eggs as they set. Add the cottage cheese and continue to fold until eggs are set but still moist. Fold in bacon bits last.

- Fill skins with the egg mixture, then dust each lightly with paprika. Top with sprigs of fresh parsley to serve.

Makes 8 large skins, each about 200 calories.

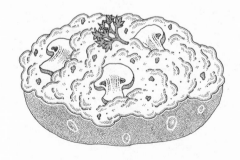

Creamy Fresh Vegetable Skins

7 large potato skins, crisped and hot using a minimum of butter

¼ cup flour
2 cups nonfat milk
¾ teaspoon salt, regular or seasoned
Fresh black pepper
1 cup grated cheddar cheese
2 tablespoons diced pimento
1 teaspoon each dry mustard, Worcestershire sauce, and dry sherry
Dash of cayenne

5 cups perfectly steamed fresh vegetables, well drained (cauliflower, broccoli, carrots, mushrooms, pearl on~ions, etc. —you choose)

Topping
&
Garnish
(4 tablespoons fresh bread crumbs
(paprika

- Put the flour in a medium~size saucepan. Gradually blend in the milk until smooth and lump free. Add salt and pepper. Stir over low heat until sauce comes to a boil. Boil and stir continuously for 1 minute.

- Blend in cheese, pimento, mustard, Worcestershire, sherry and cayenne until smooth. Fold in the veggies last, and heat momentarily until all is hot and creamy.

- Spoon a generous portion of sauced vegetables into each skin. Sprinkle the crumbs evenly over the tops, and dust lightly with paprika.

- Broil until crumbs turn golden.

Makes 7 large skins, each about 150 calories.

165

Skinny Pizza Skins

Perfect pizza without all that dough.

8 large potato skins, lightly crisped using the slightest
   amount of olive oil

1 cup prepared pizza or spaghetti sauce
1 cup shredded mozzarella cheese
1 cup assorted toppings *
Grated Parmesan cheese
Fresh or dried herbs ~ basil, oregano, fennel, parsley...

*Assorted Toppings
- diced fresh tomatoes
- chopped or sliced olives
- diced onion
- sliced or chopped green bell pepper
- thinly sliced mushrooms
- bits of cooked lean ground beef, chicken, or seafood
- hot chili peppers
- etc.

Spoon prepared sauce generously over each skin. Cover
with equal amounts of mozzarella. Apply your favorite
assorted toppings, using about 2 tablespoons per skin.
Sprinkle on a little Parmesan and some herbs of your
choice.

Broil until sizzling hot, and cheese is melted and gooey.

   Makes 8 large skins, each furnishing approximately
85 delicious calories, depending on the sauce used and
the selection of toppings.

green pepper strip

pizza sauce

melted mozzarella

diced onion

sliced olive

mushroom

crispy potato "crust"

Scalloped Seafood Skins

6 large potato skins, lightly crisped using a minimum of butter

¼ cup flour
¾ teaspoon salt
Fresh black pepper
1½ cups nonfat milk
⅓ cup minced scallions
½ cup grated Swiss cheese
1 tablespoon lemon juice
¼ teaspoon dry sherry
Pinch of thyme
Dash of nutmeg

1 cup cooked shrimp
1 cup cooked flaked crab meat
1 cup diced cooked potatoes
¾ cup freshly steamed peas
2 tablespoons diced pimento

Topping & Garnish
- 2 tablespoons each grated Parmesan cheese and fresh bread crumbs
- chopped parsley
- paprika

Preheat oven to 350.° Place the flour, salt and pepper in a medium-size saucepan. Gradually blend in the milk and scallions. Cook over medium heat until sauce is thick and bubbly, stirring constantly. Continue to boil and stir 1 minute longer.

Over low heat, blend in Swiss cheese, lemon juice, sherry, thyme and nutmeg until cheese is melted. Fold in the seafood, potatoes, peas and pimento until evenly mixed.

Fill the skins with the seafood mixture. Combine the Parmesan and bread crumbs, and sprinkle over each skin. Top with parsley, and a light dusting of paprika.

Bake 20 to 25 minutes, or until thoroughly hot and topping is crispy.

Makes 6 large skins, each about 190 calories.

Ricotta Potato Soufflés

4 medium~size whole potatoes

1 teaspoon oil
1 small clove garlic, finely minced
2 tablespoons minced onion
1 cup part~skim ricotta cheese
½ cup grated Parmesan cheese
2 tablespoons chopped parsley
½ teaspoon each salt, basil and oregano
Pinch of fennel seed
Fresh black pepper
2 egg whites, stiffly beaten
~Extra Parmesan~

- Scrub potatoes, pierce each with a knife, then bake at 400° 1 to 1¼ hours, or until insides are soft and tender. Cool just enough to handle comfortably.

- Slice a thin lid off the top of each potato and carefully scoop out the innards into a large bowl, leaving the potato "shell" intact.

- Preheat oven to 375°. In hot oil, briefly sauté garlic and onion until soft. Add to potato innards and mash well. Beat in ricotta, Parmesan, parsley and seasonings until fluffy. Gently stir in the stiffly beaten egg whites until all is uniform.

- Fill potato shells with cheese mixture, mounting them as high as they will go. Shake on some extra Parmesan.

- Bake about 30 minutes, or until very hot and tops are lightly brown and crusty.

Makes 4 stuffed potatoes, about 300 calories each.

A Few Creative Variations:

—The last few minutes of oven time, top each stuffed potato with a thin slice of mozzarella cheese and bake until cheese is melted and gooey. Yum!

—Skip the final dosage of Parmesan. Top hot baked stuffed potatoes with a large tomato which has been seeded and chopped. Sprinkle on Parmesan and/or mozzarella and broil.

—Vary the filling by adding some steamed zucchini, chopped mushrooms, cooked spinach (well drained), or leftover lean meat.

Skinny Stuffed Potatoes

Just add a salad and fresh fruit for a totally guilt~free meal.

4 medium~size whole potatoes

1 cup lowfat cottage cheese
¼ cup plain yogurt
½ cup finely grated
   cheddar cheese
1 scallion, finely minced
2 tablespoons chopped parsley

2 tablespoons soy bacon bits
1 teaspoon Dijon mustard
½ teaspoon seasoned salt
¼ teaspoon curry powder
Fresh black pepper
Dash of cayenne

Topping { 2 tablespoons grated cheddar
             paprika

Garnish { dollops of plain yogurt

Scrub potatoes well, pierce each with a knife, and bake at 400° for 1¼ hours or until outsides are crusty and in~sides are soft. Cool just enough to handle.

Preheat oven to 375.° Slice off the tops of the potatoes like so ⬭, and hollow out the innards leaving a stur~dy, but relatively thin shell. (Reserve shells for the next step.) Mash the innards well with a potato masher, wire whisk, or pastry blender until lump free. Beat in the remaining ingredients except topping and garnish until fluffy and uniformly combined.

Stuff the potato shells as high as they will go with the filling. Top each with ½ tablespoon of cheddar and an ap~plication of paprika.

Bake 25 to 30 minutes, or until hot and heavenly. Garnish each with yogurt if you're so inclined.

Makes 4 stuffed potatoes, about 285 calories each.

Note: 1 cup of freshly steamed veggies can be added. Try green peas, chopped mushrooms, diced carrot or zucchini.

170

Kiddie Skins

So, you've got kids at your house. Those little humans who try our patience whenever there's an opportunity, then offer love and kisses just when we're about to pop our corks. Right? RIGHT!

All kids go through stages with their eating habits. Sometimes it seems as if they haven't eaten two bites worth of nourishing food in days, then all of a sudden their appetites zoom and your cupboards are bare (not to mention the refrigerator, too). Some kids are picky about what they eat, while others will eat anything and everything. One thing is for certain: All kids love "fun foods"— foods they can crunch, munch, eat on the go, and put catsup on. Potato skins fall effortlessly into that category.

When vegetables are thoughtfully cooked, piled into crispy potato skins and topped with melted cheese, little noses don't turn up as often. You can top mini-size skins with a mild filling and give them to a small child as finger food he or she can eat without assistance.

In this chapter you will find some very simple recipes using foods your children already adore. Now is the time to rid your kids of the junk food habit and get them into the potato skin habit. Warning: Once they're hooked, it's a tough habit to break.

Coney Island Burger Skins

A real treat, especially when served with buttery corn on the cob and fresh watermelon chunks.

6 medium~size potato skins, lightly crisped

1 lb. lean ground beef

8 oz. mild cheddar or American cheese, sliced

Toppings & Garnishes
- catsup or barbecue sauce
- mustard
- relish or pickle slices
- chopped sweet onion

- Form ground beef into 6 hot dog~shaped cylinders. Brown in a skillet on all sides until meat is cooked but still juicy inside. Drain on paper towels, then place a "burger dog" into each skin.

- Cut up the cheese slices and tuck them around the "burger dogs" (or lay them in strips across the top). Secure with wooden toothpicks stuck through the sides, if necessary.

- Broil until cheese is melted and all is hot. Remove picks before serving, and top each skin with catsup, mustard, relish and onion.

Makes 6 medium~size skins.

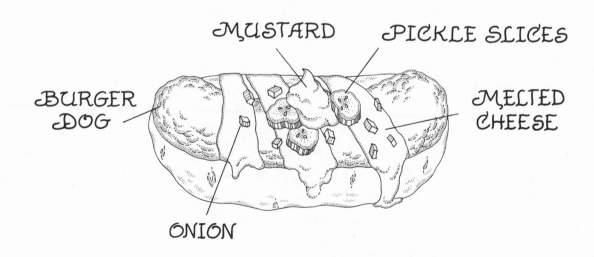

MUSTARD   PICKLE SLICES

BURGER DOG   MELTED CHEESE

ONION

Hot Dog & Bean Skins

5 or 6 medium~size potato skins, crisped or fried

1 1~lb. can pork and beans
4 hot dogs, thinly sliced on diagonal
2 tablespoons very finely minced onion
1 teaspoon prepared mustard
1 8~oz. can sliced pineapple, drained

Topping
&
Garnish
{ reserved pineapple slices
2 tablespoons packed brown sugar

- In a small saucepan, gently heat together pork and beans, hot dogs, onion and mustard. Cut 2 slices of the pineapple into small pieces. Add them to the bean mixture and continue to heat until thoroughly hot.

- Cut the remaining 2 slices pineapple into 5 or 6 pieces. Fill each skin with the bean mixture. Top with reserved pineapple pieces. Sprinkle surfaces with brown sugar.

- Broil until sugar melts.

Makes 5 or 6 medium~size skins.

Quick Pepperoni (or Hot Dog) Pizza Skins

6 medium~size potato skins, lightly crisped

3/4 cup prepared pizza sauce

1 cup shredded mozzarella cheese

1 medium~size tomato, diced

18 thin slices pepperoni or 2 hot dogs, sliced

Topping & Garnish { grated Parmesan cheese
oregano

🥚 Preheat oven to 400°. Lay the skins on a flat baking tray. Spoon 2 tablespoons sauce into each skin, followed by a generous portion of mozzarella. Place some chopped to~mato on top of each, then about 3 slices of pepperoni (or hot dog). Sprinkle the skins with some Parmesan and a little oregano.

🥚 Bake about 15 minutes, or until mozzarella is melted and skins are thoroughly hot. Yum !!

Makes 6 medium~size skins.

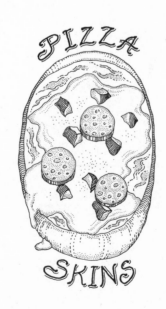

174

Crispy Fish Stick Skins

4 medium~size potato skins, crisped or fried and hot
Mayonnaise
1 cup shredded lettuce
8 average~size frozen fish sticks, cooked and hot *
Catsup
8 dill pickle slices

Into each hot skin, spread a little mayonnaise. Top with about ¼ cup lettuce, followed by 2 fish sticks. Drizzle on a little catsup, and garnish each with a pickle slice.

Makes 4 medium~size skins.

*Bake the fish sticks according to package directions.

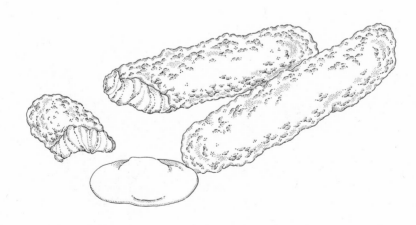

175

Crisp~Baked Skins with Catsup, Barbecue, Sour Cream & Salsa

These are sure to keep them busy.

9 mini potato skins, crisped and hot *
Salt
Catsup, barbecue sauce, sour cream and mild chunky salsa

Sprinkle each hot potato skin with a little salt. Serve in a napkin~lined basket accompanied by small unbreakable containers of catsup, barbecue, sour cream and salsa for dipping or spreading.

Makes 9 mini skins — enough for about 3 kids.

* Cook any amount of potato skins you desire. Make more if you're serving a crowd or if the kiddies are known to have hefty appetites.

Sloppy Jessie Skins

Sweeter and more delicious than Sloppy Joes.

6 medium to large potato skins, crisped or fried and hot
1 tablespoon oil
1 lb. lean ground beef
1 onion, chopped
1 medium-size green bell pepper, diced
1 clove garlic, crushed
1 1-lb. can tomatoes, undrained
3 tablespoons catsup
1 tablespoon each prepared mustard and dark brown
    sugar
1 teaspoon each chili powder and salt
Fresh black pepper
2 whole cloves
1 bay leaf

Topping
&
Garnish
{ ½ cup corn chips
{ pickle slices

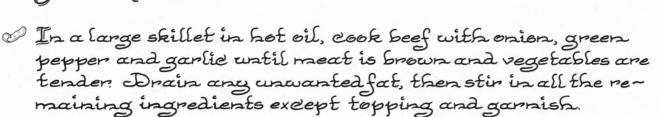

- In a large skillet in hot oil, cook beef with onion, green pepper and garlic until meat is brown and vegetables are tender. Drain any unwanted fat, then stir in all the remaining ingredients except topping and garnish.

- Bring mixture to a gentle boil, crushing the tomatoes into little pieces. Simmer, partially covered, about 30 minutes, or until thick and chunky—stirring very often.

- Remove bay leaf. Stuff the skins generously with the beef mixture. Top each with a few corn chips and some pickle slices.

Makes 6 medium to large skins.

Toasty Dog Skins

Be sure _NOT_ to crisp or fry the skins first.

Bacon Toasty Dogs

4 large potato skins
4 hot dogs
4 slices bacon

Toppings & Garnishes {
barbecue sauce or catsup
chopped onion
mustard
pickle slices or relish

▢ Preheat oven to 400°. Fit a hot dog lengthwise into each skin. Bring the sides together, and wrap each stuffed skin tightly with a bacon slice. Secure with toothpicks stuck through the sides.

▢ Bake them on a broiler rack (so fat drains), turning frequently until bacon is nicely cooked—about 30 minutes.

▢ Remove picks and serve with any of the above toppings and garnishes.

Makes 4 Toasty Dogs, or 4 servings.

Cheese Toasty Dogs

4 large potato skins
4 hot dogs
4 slices of your most favorite cheese

Toppings & Garnishes {see above suggestions

▢ Preheat oven to 400°. Make a few diagonal slashes across the surface of each hot dog. (Do not cut all the way through.) Place your "dogs" into their skins. Cut the cheese slices to fit snugly around the "dogs." Secure with wooden toothpicks stuck through the sides.

▢ Bake them for about 20 minutes (without turning), or until hot dogs are brown, cheese is melted, and everything is sizzling.

▢ Remove the picks and serve with the above toppings and garnishes.

Makes 4 Toasty Dogs, or 4 servings.

Mexican Taco Skins

Kids adore these. Better make lots.

6 medium to large potato skins, crisped or fried and hot

1 tablespoon oil
1 lb. lean ground beef
1 medium~size onion, diced
1 clove garlic, crushed
1 large tomato, chopped
1 teaspoon each oregano, chili powder and sugar
¾ teaspoon salt
½ teaspoon cumin
Fresh black pepper

Topping
&
Garnish
{
1 heaping cup (packed) shredded lettuce
1 cup grated mild cheddar cheese
tortilla chips
mild taco sauce
}

▷ In hot oil in a medium~size saucepan, brown beef with onion and garlic until meat is no longer pink. Add the tomato and all the seasonings. Simmer, uncovered, about 10 minutes, or until thick and flavorful—stirring frequently.

▷ Spoon a layer of meat mixture into each skin. Follow with a neat pile of lettuce and some grated cheese. Top each with tortilla chips (1 or 2) and a little taco sauce. Serve hot.

Makes 6 medium to large skins.

Pigs in a Blanket

Everything kids love to eat.

4 medium-size potatoes

¼ cup each mayonnaise and sour cream
2 teaspoons prepared mustard
2 teaspoons grated onion
½ teaspoon seasoned salt
Fresh black pepper

4 hot dogs, cooked (or substitute cooked sausage links)

Topping { 4 oz. cheddar cheese, sliced
paprika

Garnish { pickle slices or relish
catsup

- Bake the potatoes in the usual fashion for about 1 hour, or until done. Cool until handleable. Preheat oven to 350°.

- Cut a slice off the top of each potato, and scoop out the innards into a bowl, leaving a nice shell. Mash the innards, then beat in the mayo, sour cream, mustard, onion and seasonings until smooth and lump-free. Spoon the innards back into the potato shells. Press a cooked hot dog lengthwise into each stuffed potato.

- Bake them about 15 to 20 minutes, or until thoroughly hot. Remove potatoes from oven. Lay cheese slices on top, and sprinkle with paprika. Bake for another 5 minutes or so—until cheese is melted.

- Serve the "Pigs" hot, topped with pickle slices or relish. Pass around the catsup.

Makes 4 large kiddie servings.

(For small eaters, cut each potato in half crosswise to serve 8.)

180

Wonderful Ways with Potato Innards

You could probably sculpt a potato castle or construct a floating potato boat out of those tasty innards. But honestly, wouldn't you rather savor a large helping of potato kugel, or bite into a hearty dumpling or crispy potato pancake? I think so.

This chapter will add a new dimension to those ordinary potato side dishes you're accustomed to serving. While you prepare to stuff those crispy potato skins for tomorrow night's supper, you can begin to incorporate their scooped-out innards into another culinary masterpiece. Just read on for a marvelous selection of potato recipes you'll find totally irresistible.

Here are two tips that may come in handy when you are preparing a Potato Innard recipe:

1. If a recipe calls for dices, slices, or gratings of cooked potatoes (as in salads, scalloped dishes and kugels), chill the potato innards first. The cold potatoes will be much easier to cut or grate. Use a small sharp knife for the best control.

2. The opposite is true for recipes requiring you to mash the potatoes. Warm them first (a double boiler or microwave oven is helpful) before mashing. This will dry and soften the potato innards and prevent lumpiness. Get a good sturdy masher, too.

Potato & Ham Croquettes in Swiss Mustard Sauce

Quite a filling dish. Serve with broiled tomato halves and a healthy green salad.

4 cups cubed cooked potatoes
½ cup each grated Swiss cheese and minced ham
¼ cup finely minced onion
1 tablespoon chopped parsley
½ teaspoon seasoned salt
Fresh black pepper

Flour
2 beaten eggs
¾ cup dry bread crumbs

Oil for deep fat frying
Swiss Mustard Sauce (recipe follows)
~Paprika~

- Put the potatoes through a ricer into a large bowl. Combine with cheese, ham, onion, parsley, seasoned salt and pepper.

- With floured hands, shape potato mixture into 16 croquettes, each about the size and shape of a small, slender egg. Coat the croquettes lightly with flour, dip into beaten eggs, then roll in bread crumbs to coat completely.

- Heat a 1-inch pool of oil to 365°. Fry croquettes until crisp and well browned on all sides. Drain briefly on paper towels, then place on a warm platter.

- To serve: Pour the Swiss Mustard Sauce directly over the croquettes, then sprinkle the top lightly with paprika.

Makes 4 servings.

Swiss Mustard Sauce:

2 tablespoons butter
2 tablespoons flour
1¼ cups milk
¼ teaspoon salt
Fresh black pepper
Dash cayenne
½ cup shredded Swiss cheese
1 teaspoon prepared mustard
½ cup freshly steamed peas (kept warm)

● In a small saucepan, melt butter. Remove from heat and blend in flour. Gradually stir in the milk until smooth. Add salt, pepper and cayenne.

● Bring the sauce to a boil, stirring constantly. Continue to boil and stir for 1 minute longer, or until thick and smooth. Remove from heat and blend in cheese, mustard and peas.

Scalloped Potatoes Lorraine

4 slices bacon, diced
1 medium~size onion, thinly sliced
1 clove garlic, crushed
¾ teaspoon salt
¼ teaspoon each nutmeg and black pepper
2 eggs
1 cup half~and~half
⅔ cup sour cream, room temperature
4 cups sliced cooked potatoes
1½ cups grated Swiss cheese
1 tablespoon butter

☞ Preheat oven to 375.° Lightly butter a 2~quart casserole or baking dish. In a small skillet, sauté bacon with onion and garlic until bacon is crisp and onion is soft, stirring frequently. Drain well on paper toweling and set aside.

☞ Mix together salt, nutmeg and pepper; set aside. In a me~dium~size bowl, beat eggs with half~and~half and sour cream until uniformly combined.

☞ Now for the layers: In the prepared casserole, layer ⅓ of the potato slices followed by ½ of the bacon/onion mixture. Sprinkle with ⅓ of the seasonings and top with ⅓ of the grated cheese. Cover with another ⅓ of the potato slices, the remaining bacon/onion mixture, and another ⅓ each of the seasonings and cheese. At last, a final dosage of potatoes sprinkled with remaining seasonings and cheese. Pour beaten egg mixture over all. Dot the top with bits of butter.

☞ Bake uncovered, for approximately 1 hour, or until sur~face is golden brown. For an even crispier surface, broil briefly under close watch. Let casserole stand a couple of minutes before spooning out.

Makes 6 satisfying servings.

Mexican Hash Brown Cake

Hash browns turned into a fiesta!

4 cups packed shredded cooked potatoes
1 small onion, diced
1 small green bell pepper, diced
1 small red bell pepper, diced
1 clove garlic, crushed
½ cup finely cubed cheddar cheese
½ teaspoon seasoned salt
¼ teaspoon each cumin and oregano
Fresh black pepper
A few dashes cayenne (to taste)
2 tablespoons each butter and oil

Garnishes { sour cream
{ sliced black olives

☁ In a large bowl, gently toss potatoes with all ingredients except butter, oil and garnishes.

☁ Melt butter and oil together in a heavy 10~inch skillet (prefer~ably non~stick). Add potato mixture. Cook over medium heat, stirring frequently, about 10 minutes. (Cheese will melt nicely.)

☁ With a large spoon or spatula, press potato mixture into a flat cake and sprinkle with 2 tablespoons water. Cover skil~let and cook over low heat (in complete privacy) 10 to 15 min~utes longer, or until bottom is crusty and brown.

☁ Place an inverted serving plate on top of skillet. Invert po~tato cake onto plate, crusty side up. (Make certain the bottom isn't at all stuck to the skillet.) Spoon some sour cream decoratively into the center of the cake and sprin~kle with sliced olives.

Makes 4 to 6 servings.

Dilled Potato Soufflé

A very tasty brunch, lunch or supper dish.

4 cups cooked peeled potato chunks
3/4 cup half-and-half, warmed
1/2 cup freshly grated Parmesan cheese
1/4 cup finely minced scallions
1 teaspoon seasoned salt
1/2 teaspoon dill weed
1/4 teaspoon dry mustard
Fresh black pepper
3 eggs, separated and at room temperature
(Optional: Crumbled cooked bacon or soy bacon bits)

Topping { melted butter
extra Parmesan
paprika

Garnish { spoonfuls of sour cream

- Preheat oven to 375°. With a food processor, a beater, or a strong arm, whip potatoes until smooth and fluffy. Gradually add half-and-half, beating well to incorporate all the liquid. Blend in 1/2 cup Parmesan, scallions and seasonings until uniform. Thoroughly stir in egg yolks and optional bacon bits; set aside.

- In a small bowl, beat egg whites to stiff peaks. Carefully fold egg whites into potato mixture. Pour into an ungreased 1 1/2 ~ quart soufflé or deep casserole dish. With a very light hand, brush the top of the soufflé with melted butter, then sprinkle with extra Parmesan and paprika.

- Bake about 45 minutes or so, until top is golden brown. Top each portion with a spoonful of cool sour cream.

Makes 6 servings.

Hint: Warm cooked potatoes will beat to a smoother consis~tency more quickly than cold potatoes.

186

Potato~Sausage Fritters

Try them with eggs for a leisurely Sunday breakfast.

2½ cups finely diced cooked potatoes
1 cup crumbled cooked sausage (Italian or country~style)
¼ cup finely minced onion
1 tablespoon chopped parsley
2 egg yolks
3 tablespoons half~and~half or milk
¼ cup flour
¼ teaspoon seasoned salt
Fresh black pepper
2 egg whites, beaten to stiff peaks
2 to 4 tablespoons Parmesan cheese

Oil for frying

Accompaniments: catsup and
                grated Parmesan

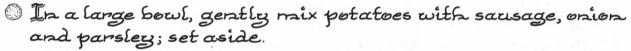

- In a large bowl, gently mix potatoes with sausage, onion and parsley; set aside.

- In a small bowl, whisk together egg yolks, half~and~half, flour, seasoned salt and pepper until smooth. Fold yolk mixture into beaten egg whites until uniformly combined. Gently but thoroughly fold the egg batter into potato mix~ture, adding 2 to 4 tablespoons of Parmesan.

- Heat ¼ to ½ inch of oil in a large, heavy skillet. Drop the potato batter by heaping tablespoons into hot oil, frying each side until nicely brown and crisp. Remove fritters with a slotted spoon onto paper toweling to drain well.

- Serve on a warm platter, with lots of catsup for dunking and a shaker of Parmesan for sprinkling.

Makes about 20 fritters, or 4 to 6 servings.

Potato & Onion Soup Fondue
with French Bread Croutons

I hate to boast, but this recipe is fantastic!

2 tablespoons <u>each</u> butter and oil
2 cups thinly sliced onions, lightly packed
2 cloves garlic, finely minced
2 cups chicken stock
1 teaspoon salt
Fresh black pepper } to taste
Cayenne
4 cups diced cooked potatoes

1½ cups milk
1 cup heavy (whipping) cream
1 cup grated Jack cheese

French Bread Croutons (recipe follows)

Melt butter and oil together in a large saucepan. Sauté onions and garlic until very soft—don't burn them. Add the stock, salt, black pepper, cayenne and potatoes. Bring to a gentle boil, then cover and simmer for 10 minutes.

Cool mixture slightly, then purée the entire thing in a blender. (Better do this in 2 or 3 batches.) Return the purée to the saucepan and whisk in the milk and cream. Stir over low heat just until hot. Blend in the cheese until melted.

To serve, top each bowlful generously with French Bread Croutons.

Makes 4 to 6 servings.

188

French Bread Croutons:

3 to 4 (¾ inch thick) slices good French bread or sourdough
    French bread
2 tablespoons butter, softened
1 small clove garlic, very finely minced
Grated Parmesan cheese

Cut the bread in ¾ inch thick slices (if you haven't already done so). Lay them on a broiler pan. Cream together butter and garlic. Spread one side of each slice of bread with some of the butter mixture. Sprinkle on a nice layer of Parmesan.

Broil until surfaces become very light brown and crisp, watching closely. Turn bread, then repeat the butter~Parmesan~broiling routine with side #2.

Gently grip your perfectly toasted bread with one hand as you cut them into large cubes with the other hand, using a serrated knife and sawing motion.

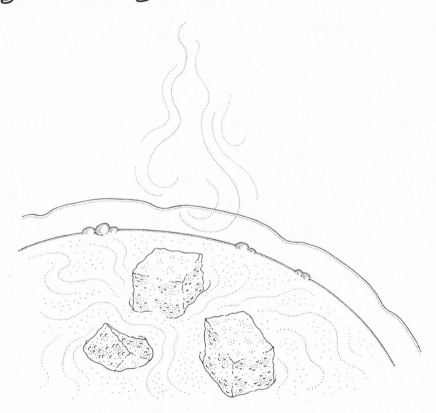

Creamy Seafood Chowder

Serve from your best tureen, with hot homemade biscuits.

4 slices bacon, diced
1 cup chopped onion
1 cup sliced mushrooms
1 small clove garlic, finely minced (optional)
¾ cup fresh or frozen peas
1 cup water
1¾ teaspoons seasoned salt
Fresh black pepper

4 cups half-and-half
¼ cup butter
¼ cup flour
1 cup clam juice
2 cups chopped clams (about 4 6½-oz. cans — drain, reserving clam juice)
1 cup cooked shrimp
3 to 4 cups cubed cooked potatoes
2 tablespoons diced pimento

~Fresh chopped parsley~

In a large kettle or saucepan, sauté bacon with onion, mushrooms, garlic and peas until onion is tender and flavors mingle. Add water, salt and pepper, and bring to a gentle boil. Cover and simmer about 10 minutes, or until peas are just tender.

Add the half-and-half and butter. Stir over low heat until hot — do not boil. Combine the flour and clam juice, and blend this into the soup. Stir patiently, until it thickens slightly.

Now add the clams, shrimp, potatoes and pimento, and continue to stir over low heat until the soup is hot and creamy. Turn off the heat, cover the kettle, and let the soup sit for a few solitary minutes before serving (for extra creaminess and sumptuous flavor).

Ladle into soup bowls, and garnish each portion with fresh parsley.

Makes 8 servings.

Idea: You may add bits of other seafood as well. Try scallops, chunks of crab or even lobster. Leftover pieces of cooked fish work well; snapper, halibut, etc.

190

Succotash Chowder

A soothing dish to warm you inside, and put a smile on your face.

4 slices bacon, diced
1 medium~size onion, chopped
3 cups fresh or frozen corn
1 cup frozen lima beans
1 cup water

2 cups milk
1 cup half~and~half
1 cup heavy (whipping) cream
¼ cup butter
2 teaspoons each salt and sugar
Fresh black pepper
Dash cayenne
4 cups cubed cooked potatoes
1½ cups grated Jack cheese, packed
~Paprika~

🫘 In a large kettle, sauté bacon with onion until onion is soft and bacon is partially cooked. Add corn and limas, and stir over medium heat for 2 minutes. Add water, cover the kettle, and simmer gently for 10 minutes, or until the veggies are tender.

🫘 Uncover, and add all the remaining ingredients except paprika. Stir over low heat until soup is thoroughly hot—do not boil.

🫘 Turn off the heat, cover the kettle, and allow the soup to "re~lax" for a few quiet minutes before serving. (This will heighten the flavor and give it extra creaminess.)

🫘 Ladle the soup into large bowls and dust each serving lightly with paprika.

Makes 8 to 10 servings.

Dilled Potato~Leek Chowder

Soothing on a cold winter's night.

4 tablespoons butter
3 cups thinly sliced leeks
1 cup thinly sliced celery
1 medium~size carrot, diced
1 cup chicken stock

2 cups milk
1 cup half~and~half
3 tablespoons flour
¾ teaspoon seasoned salt
¼ teaspoon dill weed
Fresh black pepper
2 cups diced cooked potatoes

Various Garnishes
{ chopped fresh parsley
extra dill weed
crisply cooked and crumbled bacon or soy bacon bits
chopped fresh mushrooms and parsley sprigs

Melt butter in a large saucepan; sauté leeks, celery and carrot until vegetables become soft. Add stock; cover and simmer over low heat for 10 to 15 minutes, stirring periodically.

Gradually stir in the milk. Make a smooth mixture of the half~and~half and flour (do this by slowly blending the half~and~half into the flour) and stir this into the soup. Add the seasoned salt, dill weed, pepper and potatoes. Continue to stir over low heat until the soup barely comes to a boil—be patient. It will thicken nicely. Now, taste for any additional seasoning.

Ladle into soup bowls and garnish to your liking.

Makes 4 to 6 warming servings.

Savory Potato Pancakes

A nice surprise for Sunday breakfast.

4 cups packed shredded cooked potatoes
1/3 cup minced onion (you may substitute scallions)
3 tablespoons flour
2 to 3 tablespoons crumbled cooked bacon or soy bacon bits
1 teaspoon seasoned salt
Fresh black pepper
1 egg
Butter, oil, or bacon drippings

- In a large bowl, gently (but thoroughly) toss together potatoes, onion, flour, bacon, salt and pepper; set aside.

- In a small bowl, beat egg until thick and light; fold into potato mixture until evenly incorporated.

- Form potato mixture into 8 large pancakes. Heat a thin layer of butter, oil, or drippings in a large heavy skillet. Fry the cakes 5 to 7 minutes, or until they are crisp and brown, turning once. Press them down with a spatula as you cook. (Go light on oil, using just enough to keep cakes from sticking and to make a crisp outer coating.)

- Serve hot, with chunky cinnamon applesauce and sour cream.

Makes 8 potato pancakes.

sour cream

chunky cinnamon applesauce

Savory Potato Pancakes

Sour Cream Scalloped Potatoes

Two crispy toppings to choose from!

3 tablespoons butter
1 cup thinly sliced mushrooms
3 tablespoons flour
1½ cups half-and-half
½ teaspoon salt
Fresh black pepper

Dash each cayenne and nutmeg
½ cup sour cream, room temperature
2 teaspoons dry sherry
4 cups sliced cooked potatoes
¼ cup thinly sliced scallions

Topping #1 { ¼ cup toasted sliced almonds
grated Parmesan cheese

Topping #2 { ¼ cup dry bread crumbs
2 tablespoons grated Parmesan cheese
½ tablespoon melted butter
1 tablespoon chopped parsley

Preheat oven to 325°. Butter a 2-quart casserole or its equivalent. In a medium-size saucepan melt 3 tablespoons butter; sauté mushrooms until tender. Sprinkle in the flour as you stir; cook until mixture is very thick. Remove pan from heat and slowly blend in half-and-half until mixture is smooth and free of lumps (except for the mushrooms, of course).

Return saucepan to medium-low heat and blend in salt, pepper, cayenne and nutmeg. Stir continuously until sauce comes to a boil, then boil and stir 1 minute longer. Remove from heat and blend in sour cream and sherry until smooth. Fold in potatoes and scallions.

Pour sauce mixture into the prepared casserole and apply one of the toppings. For Topping #1, sprinkle on almonds and Parmesan; for Topping #2, toss together all ingredients and sprinkle over top of casserole.

Bake, uncovered, until all is hot — about 15 minutes.

Makes 6 incredible servings.

Cottage Fried Potatoes & Bacon

A traditional potato dish—nice with scrambled eggs and fresh coffee.

2 tablespoons butter
2 tablespoons oil or bacon drippings
4 heaping cups sliced cooked potatoes
½ cup minced onion
¼ cup minced red and/or green bell peppers
1 teaspoon seasoned salt
Fresh black pepper
2 slices bacon, crisply cooked and crumbled or 2 table-
    spoons soy bacon bits

Various Accompaniments: sour cream
                        catsup
                        grated Parmesan

In a large, heavy skillet, heat together butter and oil (or drippings) until hot. Layer the potatoes artfully in the skil-let, exposing as much potato surface to the butter/oil mix-ture as possible. Sprinkle on the onion, pepper(s), seasoned salt and black pepper.

Cook over low heat until the bottom layer of potatoes be-comes brown and crisp. (Shake the pan often to keep them from sticking.) With a large spatula, turn the potatoes in batches and brown the other side. Sprinkle on the bacon and gently toss potato mixture the last few minutes of cooking—until all is crisp and flavorful.

To serve: Place the potato mixture on a warm platter and pass around the accompaniments.

Makes 4 to 6 servings.

Potato Salad Olé

Perfect with cold chicken and crispy tortilla chips on a warm afternoon.

6 cups cubed cooked potatoes
1 cup shredded cheddar cheese
½ cup <u>each</u> diced red and green bell peppers
½ cup sliced black olives
¼ cup minced onion
1 firm tomato, seeded and diced
1 cup mayonnaise
¼ cup sour cream
2 tablespoons diced green chilies
2 tablespoons lemon juice
½ teaspoon salt
¼ teaspoon cumin
Fresh black pepper
A few dashes of chili powder

Garnishes { 1 avocado, pitted and thinly sliced
fresh cilantro (or parsley) sprigs

chips
avocado
sour cream
olive
potato salad
jalapeño

In a large mixing bowl, combine all ingredients in order listed, except for the garnishes. Stir gently to moisten everything evenly. Heap the potato mixture into a nice serving bowl.

To garnish, lay the avocado slices, spoke-fashion, on top of the potato salad with a few cilantro sprigs in the center. Chill well before serving.

Makes 6 to 8 servings.

More garnishing ideas: ≈ tortilla chips
≈ salsa (mild to hot)
≈ jalapeño peppers
≈ whole black olives
≈ sour cream
≈ grated cheddar

Creamy Potato & Shrimp Salad

4 cups cubed cooked potatoes
1 cup cooked shrimp (or flaked crab meat)
2 stalks celery, chopped
½ cup minced onion
2 tablespoons sliced pimento~stuffed olives
1 hard~cooked egg, chopped

½ cup mayonnaise
2 tablespoons each sour cream and sweet pickle relish,
   drained
1 tablespoon catsup or chili sauce
1 tablespoon chopped pimento~stuffed olives
1 hard~cooked egg, chopped
2 teaspoons each lemon juice and sugar
¼ teaspoon paprika
Salt and pepper

~Freshly chopped parsley~
~Tomato wedges~

- In a large bowl, combine potatoes with shrimp, celery, onion, 2 tablespoons sliced olives, and one of the chopped eggs.

- In a small bowl, stir together remaining ingredients except salt, pepper, the parsley and tomato wedges. Fold this dress~ing gently into the potato mixture, moistening everything nicely. Add salt and pepper to taste.

- Spoon the salad into a serving bowl. Sprinkle the top with chopped parsley and decorate with tomato wedges. Chill until very cold.

Makes 4 to 6 servings.

Curried Potato Salad

4 cups cubed cooked potatoes
¾ cup thinly sliced or chopped celery
½ cup diced red peppers
½ cup sliced scallions (whites and greens)
½ cup cooked garbanzo beans
⅓ cup golden raisins
¼ cup chopped toasted peanuts

½ cup mayonnaise
¼ cup sour cream
2 tablespoons firm yogurt (plain)
1½ teaspoons fresh lemon juice
1 teaspoon each curry powder and sugar
¼ teaspoon dry mustard
Salt and pepper

~ Romaine leaves ~
~ Chopped toasted peanuts ~
~ Shredded coconut ~

- In a large bowl, gently combine potatoes with celery, red peppers, scallions, garbanzos, raisins and ¼ cup peanuts.
- In a separate bowl, make the dressing: Stir mayonnaise with sour cream, yogurt, lemon juice, curry, sugar, and mustard. Fold this into the bowl of vegetables, moistening everything evenly. Taste. Season with salt and pepper to your liking.
- Line a serving bowl with romaine leaves. Spoon in the potato salad. In the center, sprinkle on some peanuts. Sprinkle a layer of coconut alongside the edge. Chill well before serving.

Makes 4 to 6 servings.

Optional additions: 1 or 2 hard-cooked eggs (chopped); a handful of fresh raw green peas.

Ham & Swiss Potato Salad

Will get rave reviews at your next picnic.

6 cups cubed cooked potatoes
1 cup diced celery
1 cup Swiss cheese, cut into small cubes
1 cup diced smoked ham
¼ cup minced onion

½ cup each sour cream and mayonnaise
½ cup sweet pickle relish, well drained
1½ tablespoons vinegar
1½ teaspoons prepared mustard
¾ teaspoon salt
Fresh black pepper
~Chopped parsley~

🥄 In a large bowl, gently combine potatoes with celery, cheese, ham and onion.

🥄 In a separate bowl, make a dressing: Stir together all remaining ingredients (except the parsley) until well mixed. Fold the dressing into the potato mixture, stirring until all elements are well coated.

🥄 Pile into a large serving bowl, and sprinkle with chopped parsley. Chill well before serving.

Makes 10 to 12 hefty servings.

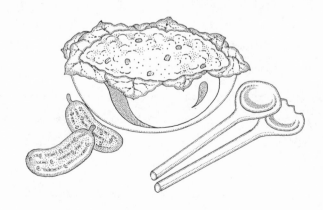

Oriental Potato Salad

Chinese vegetables combined with potatoes in a light soy dressing.

Part A
- 4 cups cubed cooked potatoes
- 1 cup celery, sliced thinly on the diagonal
- 1 cup mung bean sprouts
- 1 cup very finely shredded cabbage
- ½ cup each thinly sliced Chinese pea pods and mushrooms
- 2 large scallions, sliced on the diagonal
- ½ cup sliced water chestnuts
- ¼ cup chopped lightly toasted cashews
- 1 to 2 tablespoons lightly toasted sesame seeds

Part B
- ¼ cup salad oil
- 2 tablespoons soy sauce
- 1 tablespoon sugar or honey
- 1 tablespoon catsup
- 1 teaspoon dry sherry
- ¼ teaspoon Chinese sesame oil
- ⅛ teaspoon each crushed garlic and grated fresh ginger
- ⅛ teaspoon dry mustard

Salt and pepper to taste

~Chow mein noodles~

In a large bowl, carefully toss together all ingredients in "Part A" (the salad).

In a screw-top container, shake together well all ingredients in "Part B" (the dressing).

Lightly drizzle the dressing into the salad, gently stirring with a spatula until all the salad elements are lightly coated. Taste. Add salt and pepper if you choose. Refrigerate until cold.

Before serving, sprinkle on some crisp chow mein noodles.

200

Makes 6 to 8 servings.

<u>A suggestion</u>: For even more substance, toss in strips of cooked chicken or chunks of diced firm tofu.

<u>A note</u>: Make sure all your veggies are crisp and dry, or you may dilute the dressing.

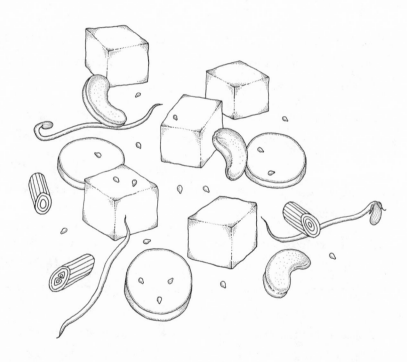

Bacon & Swiss Hash Brown Kugel

6 slices bacon, diced
½ cup chopped scallions
4 eggs, beaten
4 cups coarsely shredded or diced cooked potatoes
1 cup packed shredded Swiss cheese
½ teaspoon seasoned salt
Fresh black pepper
Dash cayenne

Garnish {lots of sour cream

- Preheat oven to 325°. Sauté bacon and scallions together until bacon begins to brown and scallions are tender. Drain well on paper toweling, reserving drippings.

- In a large bowl, combine beaten eggs with potatoes, cheese, salt, pepper and cayenne. Add drained bacon mixture.

- With a pastry brush, coat the inside of an 8-cup ring mold or round casserole with reserved bacon drippings. Pack potato mixture into mold.

- Bake for 1 to 1¼ hours, or until firm and top is crusty and golden. Carefully drain off drippings, if necessary, and loosen kugel from mold with a sharp knife. Let set a min- ute or two before inverting onto a large platter. Top each serving with a large spoonful of sour cream. Or serve kugel straight from the casserole, cut into large wedges. Top each serving with a large spoonful of sour cream.

Makes 6 servings.

Serving suggestion: Fill the baked kugel ring with creamy scrambled eggs or sautéed cherry tomatoes for a welcome brunch or supper entrée.

Italian Potato Dumplings

3½ cups riced or very well
    mashed cooked potatoes
½ cup grated Parmesan cheese
¼ cup minced scallions
¼ teaspoon finely minced garlic
1 cup flour

1 teaspoon salt
½ teaspoon basil, crushed
2 tablespoons chopped pars~
    ley
Fresh black pepper
2 eggs, beaten

About 6 oz. mozzarella cheese, cut into 20 cubes
~Extra flour~

Crispy Topping { melted butter
                   extra Parmesan

Garnish { chopped parsley

○ In a large bowl, mix potatoes with ½ cup Parmesan, scallions, garlic, flour, salt, basil, 2 tablespoons parsley and pepper. Beat in eggs until mixture forms a dough.

○ With floured hands, shape dough into 20 large balls of uniform size. Make a hole in center of each ball, press a cheese cube into each hole, then reshape into balls again, sealing in the cheese. Roll cheese~filled balls in flour just to coat them lightly.

○ Bring a large pot of salted water to a boil. Gradually drop in dumplings, stir twice, then simmer uncovered for about 15 minutes.

○ Immediately remove cooked dumplings to a buttered baking dish with a slotted spoon. Drizzle them generously with melted butter and sprinkle on lots of Parmesan. Broil until golden brown and crispy, turning them carefully in their butter and sprinkling with more Parmesan as they broil to crispen all sides. Sprinkle dumplings with chopped parsley.

○ Serve them hot, on a bed of steamed veggies (such as peas, spinach, or broccoli) with or without the addition of a tomato sauce or cream sauce.

Makes 4 to 5 wonderful servings.

Corned Beef Hash & Eggs

Makes great use of leftovers.

2½ cups diced cooked potatoes
2 cups chopped cooked corned beef
½ cup minced onion
¼ cup minced red and green bell peppers
¾ teaspoon salt
Fresh black pepper
¼ cup butter
6 eggs
¾ cup shredded Jack cheese

~Chopped parsley~
~Catsup, mild salsa, or bottled chili sauce~

- In a large bowl, toss together potatoes, corned beef, onion, peppers, salt, and black pepper to taste.

- In a large heavy skillet, melt butter. Turn the potato mixture into the skillet, pressing down to make a large, flat cake. Cook over medium heat until crusty on the bottom.

- Make 6 evenly spaced indentations in the hash. Carefully break an egg into each. Cover the skillet, and "poach" the eggs until they are set. Turn off the heat, sprinkle on the cheese, and cover the skillet once again——just until cheese is nicely melted.

- To serve: Sprinkle lightly with chopped parsley, and pass any or all of the remaining condiments.

Makes 6 servings

Potatoes Alfredo

A rich and filling potato dish.

½ cup butter
⅔ cup heavy (whipping) cream
1 cup freshly grated Parmesan cheese
¼ teaspoon salt
Fresh black pepper
4 generous cups cooked potatoes, cut into thick strips
~Fresh chopped parsley~

▱ Stir butter and cream together in a medium~size saucepan over low heat until butter melts and mixture is smooth. Re~move from heat and blend in Parmesan, salt, and a gener~ous grinding of fresh black pepper.

▱ Meanwhile, gently heat the potato strips in a covered saucepan, double boiler, or microwave oven. Carefully, but thoroughly, stir the hot potatoes into the sauce.

▱ Heap potato mixture into a warm serving bowl and sprinkle on the chopped parsley.

Makes 6 servings.

Sugar~Browned Potatoes, Apples & Raisins

A nice side dish with ribs, eggs, sausages, whatever...

4 slices bacon, cut into ½~inch pieces
1 medium~size onion, chopped
2 tart apples, peeled and coarsely chopped
½ cup golden raisins
¼ cup butter
¼ cup sugar
½ teaspoon salt
3 tablespoons water
4 cups cooked potatoes, cut into large chunks
~Cinnamon~

Garnish {yogurt (plain or honey~sweetened)
{cinnamon

In a medium~size skillet, fry bacon until crisp; drain on paper toweling, leaving bacon drippings in skillet. Sauté onion and apples in drippings until tender, stirring frequently. Mix in raisins the last minute or so of cooking. Add this sauté to the drained bacon and set aside.

In a large skillet, using a wooden spoon, melt butter, sugar and salt together. Cook over medium heat, stirring until mixture just starts to turn golden brown. Remove from heat at once and cool slightly. Thoroughly blend in the water until smooth. Add potatoes, bacon~onion~apple~ raisin mixture, and a dash of cinnamon. Stir this all together over low heat to coat everything tenderly.

Serve hot, garnishing each portion with spoonfuls of yogurt dusted with cinnamon.

Makes 4 to 6 servings.

Potato Kugel Pie Crust

2 cups packed shredded cooked potatoes
¼ cup finely minced onion
1 beaten egg
¼ teaspoon seasoned salt
Fresh black pepper
~Melted butter~

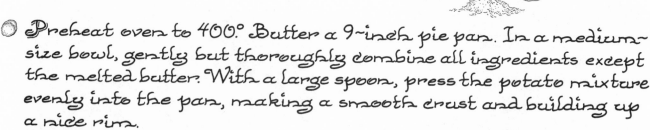

○ Preheat oven to 400°. Butter a 9~inch pie pan. In a medium-size bowl, gently but thoroughly combine all ingredients except the melted butter. With a large spoon, press the potato mixture evenly into the pan, making a smooth crust and building up a nice rim.

○ Bake the crust for 30 minutes, then remove it from the oven just to brush it lightly with the melted butter. Continue bak~ing 10 minutes or so, until lightly crisp and golden brown.

Makes 1 9~inch pie crust, ready to be filled.

<u>Other Additions Worth Considering</u>: Sunflower or sesame seeds; your favorite herbs; crumbled cooked bacon or soy bacon bits; some grated Parmesan or Romano cheese.

<u>Suggestions for Using Potato Kugel Pie Crust</u>:
≈Make a fresh vegetable pie: Into the freshly baked crust, pile on a myriad of steamed (and well drained) veggies, and top with lots of grated cheese. Broil until cheese melts. Cut into wedges.

≈Use as a base for a vegetable, meat, or seafood quiche. Especially good topped with thin slices of tomato and Parmesan.

≈How about placing some freshly steamed veggies (asparagus, cauliflower, broccoli) with wedges of hard-cooked egg upon your hot crust, then pouring on a savory cream or cheese sauce? Not a bad idea.

≈For brunch, try scrambling some eggs and onions along with bacon, ham, or sausages. Fold in lots of shredded cheese (or cream cheese), and pile into the crust. Dust with paprika.

German Potato Stuffing

Something a little different.

8 slices bacon
¼ cup butter
1½ cups each diced onion and celery
8 cups cubed cooked potatoes
1 teaspoon seasoned salt
½ teaspoon thyme
¼ teaspoon sage
Fresh black pepper
1 beaten egg
¼ cup chicken stock
4 cups dry bread cubes
¼ cup chopped parsley
1 whole egg

In a large skillet, sauté bacon in butter along with the onion and celery until bacon is partially cooked and vegetables soften. Add potatoes and seasonings, and stir gently for a couple of minutes, until everything is nicely mingled.

Pour in the beaten egg, and stir to scramble it well. Add the stock and bread cubes, and remove from heat as you fold everything together well. Stir in the parsley, then the whole raw egg to thoroughly moisten the stuffing.

Cool briefly before filling the bird, or pile the stuffing into a buttered 2-quart casserole and bake, covered, at 350° for approximately 1 hour.

Makes about 8 cups of stuffing.

Yams and Sweets

In many a household, Thanksgiving or Christmas dinner would not be complete without a generous helping of candied yams or sweet potatoes. Unfortunately, a good number of Americans only experience yams and sweet potatoes this way — but once or twice a year, served up dripping with sugar and melted marshmallows. They're tasty this way I have to agree, but there are so many more ingenious ways to prepare them. Besides, there's no good reason to reserve them for holiday fare only. That's plain neglectful, when you consider the abundance of tempting dishes presented here. Sweet potatoes and yams should be savored whenever they're in season, so what are you waiting for? The time has arrived to discover these beautiful potatoes in astonishing new ways — from the simple to the extravagant.

One final comment for you health-oriented folks: Yams and sweets are extra high in vitamin A!

Cream of Sweet Potato Soup

Something different at holiday time. Or any time.

2 tablespoons butter
2 cups chopped onion
2 cloves garlic, minced
3 cups chicken stock
2 cups mashed cooked sweet
   potatoes

In any combination to make a total of about 3 cups. All steamed until just ~ tender and drained well.

2 cups milk
1 cup heavy (whipping) cream
1 teaspoon salt
¼ teaspoon <u>each</u> cinnamon and
   ginger
Fresh black pepper
Cayenne to taste

{ Diced sweet red pepper
  Thinly sliced carrots
  Fresh green peas

Choice of garnishes { sunflower seeds, coconut
   chopped toasted nuts
   chopped parsley, paprika

- Melt butter in a large saucepan and sauté onion with garlic until very soft but not brown. Pour in the stock, then cover and simmer gently for 10 minutes.

- Blend the sweet potatoes into the simmering stock. Cool slightly, then purée the entire mixture in a blender until smooth. (Do this in 2 batches.)

- Return the purée to your saucepan, and whisk in the milk, cream, salt and spices. Cook over <u>low</u> heat just until hot, then add your perfectly steamed veggies. Cover the pan and keep hot over the lowest possible heat for 15 minutes to mingle flavors. Try not to let it boil.

- To serve, ladle the soup into bowls, and garnish with any of the suggestions above.

Makes 6 to 8 very wonderful servings.

Apricot~Almond Glazed Yams

Very sweet and simple. Marvelous with baked ham.

2 lbs. yams, cooked until just~tender, cooled and peeled

1 cup apricot preserves
⅓ cup dried apricots, cut into slivers
¼ cup <u>each</u> butter and honey
1 teaspoon grated orange peel
¼ teaspoon salt

¼ cup sliced almonds, lightly toasted

Preheat oven to 350.° Cut the yams lengthwise in half and place in a buttered baking dish or casserole; set aside.

In a small saucepan, combine preserves with slivered apricots, butter, honey, orange peel and salt. Bring to a gentle boil, stirring until butter melts and mixture forms a nice glaze.

Spoon about half of the glaze over the yams. Cover dish securely with foil, and bake for 30 minutes, basting occasionally with the extra glaze (reserving a few tablespoons for the final glazing).

Uncover the yams and bake for an additional 30 minutes, basting frequently with the hot apricot drippings (which will form in its own dish). The last 15 minutes, sprinkle on the almonds and spoon on the reserved glaze. Continue to bake until yams are well glazed.

Makes 4 to 6 servings.

Sweet & Savory Yam Cakes

2 cups raw grated peeled yam, firmly packed
1 cup grated carrot, firmly packed
¼ cup crumbled cooked bacon
3 tablespoons finely minced onion
1 clove garlic, very finely minced
4 eggs, well beaten
⅓ cup flour (white or whole wheat)
¾ teaspoon salt
Dash allspice
1 tablespoon fresh orange juice
Dash grated orange rind
Some sunflower or sesame seeds (optional, but nice)

Oil and/or butter for frying
Yogurt and/or sour cream

● Place the grated yam over a strainer and salt lightly. Let stand for 15 to 20 minutes, then press and squeeze out all the moisture. Combine in a bowl with all the remaining ingredients (except oil/butter and yogurt/sour cream), mixing well.

● Heat a thin layer of oil in a large, heavy skillet. Drop in large doses of yam mixture, shaping into 8 cakes, each about ½ inch thick. Fry slowly over low heat until very brown and crisp on both sides. (Yam needs to cook thoroughly.)

● Drain on paper towels and serve hot, with dollops of yogurt and/or sour cream.

Makes 8 nice-size cakes ～ enough to serve 4.

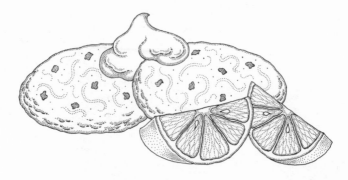

Home~Fried Sweets

4 fist~size sweet potatoes
6 slices bacon, cut into ½~inch pieces
4 tablespoons bacon drippings
Salt and pepper
Cinnamon
Pure maple syrup (optional)

- Peel raw potatoes and cut into rounds about ¼~inch thick; set aside.

- In a large heavy skillet, fry bacon until crisp, reserving all the drippings. Remove bacon to paper towels to drain, then wipe the skillet clean.

- Measure 2 tablespoons drippings back into skillet and place over low heat. Make 3 layers of potato slices, sprinkling each with a little salt, pepper, and a dash of cinnamon. Drizzle remaining drippings over all. Cover the skillet and cook slowly for about 7 to 10 minutes, or until light brown on bottom.

- Uncover, then turn potatoes with a wide spatula and brown the other side. Cook until potatoes are tender and lightly crisp. Gently toss in the cooked bacon during the last couple of minutes of frying time.

- Serve hot, as a side dish, drizzled with maple syrup and accompanied by scrambled or poached eggs.

Makes 4 Servings.

Notes: 1~ You may substitute diced ham for bacon. Sauté potatoes in a mixture of butter and oil.

2~ Try sautéing some thinly sliced fresh apple rings along with the sweets. Very aromatic with the cinnamon.

Maple Souffléed Yams with Bacon

6 egg whites, room temperature
½ teaspoon salt
¼ cup granulated sugar
2 cups mashed cooked yams
¼ cup packed brown sugar

¼ cup crisply cooked and finely crumbled bacon
½ teaspoon maple extract
Dash of cinnamon
1 cup half-and-half
~2 tablespoons very finely minced pecans~

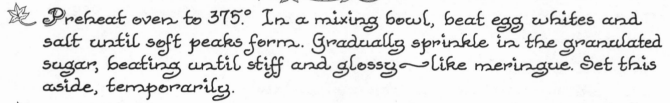

※ Preheat oven to 375°. In a mixing bowl, beat egg whites and salt until soft peaks form. Gradually sprinkle in the granulated sugar, beating until stiff and glossy—like meringue. Set this aside, temporarily.

※ In a large bowl with the same beaters (no need to wash them) beat together yams, brown sugar, bacon, maple extract and cinnamon until well blended. Scald the half-and-half in a small saucepan, then slowly beat into yam mixture until smooth and creamy. (Don't attempt to beat out the bacon lumps—they're very desirable.)

※ Gently fold egg whites into yam mixture, mixing with a rubber scraper or whisk just until evenly combined. Pour into a 2-quart soufflé or straight-sided casserole dish. Sprinkle the top with pecans.

※ Bake about 45 minutes, or until the soufflé is puffy and golden brown. Serve immediately, with a bowl of whipped butter or just by itself.

Makes 6 to 8 servings.

A suggestion: It is important for you to bring this dish directly from the oven to the dinner table, so everyone can take a look. It falls quickly, but will still taste sensational.

214

Sweet Potato Salad

Slightly exotic.

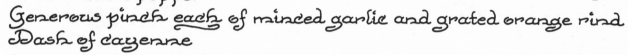

1 ½ lbs. sweet potatoes

¼ cup oil (peanut is nice)
2 tablespoons fresh orange juice
1 teaspoon honey
½ teaspoon salt
Fresh black pepper
Generous pinch <u>each</u> of minced garlic and grated orange rind
Dash of cayenne

½ cup <u>each</u> diced red and green bell peppers
1 small onion, chopped
1 stalk celery, thinly sliced
⅓ cup golden raisins
2 tablespoons chopped toasted peanuts

~ Romaine leaves ~
~ Yogurt ~
~ Toasted shredded coconut ~

◉ Boil the potatoes in their jackets until <u>just</u> tender, but not mushy. This may take anywhere from 20 to 30 minutes. Cool thoroughly, then slip off the skins. Chill the potatoes to make them firmer.

◉ Cut the potatoes into nice~size cubes and place them in a bowl. Mix the oil, juice, honey, salt, pepper, garlic, orange rind and cayenne together, then pour over the potatoes. Cover and chill thoroughly so the potatoes can absorb all the flavor.

◉ Gently stir in the peppers, onion, celery, raisins and peanuts. Toss to coat everything well. Serve on a bed of romaine leaves, topped with yogurt and coconut.

Makes 4 to 6 refreshingly different servings.

Bacon & Date Stuffed Yams

4 small yams, about 2 lbs. total
8 slices bacon, crisply fried and
   crumbled (reserve 1 tablespoon
   drippings)
⅓ cup minced onion
¼ cup sour cream
2 tablespoons butter, softened

2 tablespoons packed brown
   sugar (light or dark)
1 egg yolk
¼ teaspoon salt
⅛ teaspoon nutmeg
¼ cup finely snipped dates

Topping { extra crumbled bacon
         nutmeg
         2 tablespoons melted butter

Garnish { sour cream or yogurt (optional)

- Bake yams until tender in a 375° oven — about 45 minutes or so. Cool until handleable.

- In a small skillet in 1 tablespoon reserved bacon drippings, sauté onion until tender but not brown; set aside.

- Preheat oven to 400°. Cut a thin slice off the tops of the yams lengthwise, and gently scoop out the innards into a medium-size bowl, leaving the "shells" intact for stuffing. Mash the innards well, then beat them with the sour cream, softened butter, sugar, egg yolk, salt and nutmeg until well blended. Stir in almost all of the cooked bacon (reserving about 2 tablespoons for the topping), the sautéed onion and the dates until they are evenly distributed.

- Carefully stuff the yam shells, building the surfaces up nicely. Press the reserved bacon onto the surfaces, then sprinkle tops lightly with nutmeg. Drizzle each stuffed yam with some of the melted butter.

- Bake for approximately 20 minutes, or until yams are hot throughout. Top each with a small dollop of sour cream or yogurt.

Makes 4 servings.

Jamaican Stuffed Sweets

4 nicely shaped sweet potatoes (about 3 lbs.)
½ cup butter, softened
1 8½-oz. can crushed pineapple, well drained
2 tablespoons each golden rum and honey
½ cup chopped pecans
⅓ cup toasted coconut
½ teaspoon cardamom or allspice
¼ teaspoon salt

Topping   2 tablespoons each chopped pecans, toasted coconut,
        and packed brown sugar
        4 tablespoons melted butter

Bake the sweet potatoes in a 375° oven for 45 minutes to 1 hour, or until soft and tender. (Butter skins first and pierce them once with a knife.) Cool until handleable.

Preheat oven to 400°. Make a thin slit across the top of each potato, and carefully scoop out the innards leaving a nice whole shell to stuff. Beat the innards in a large bowl until smooth. Beat in the softened butter, then all remaining ingredients except the topping.

Stuff the shells fully, using up all the filling. (The top sides should not close together.) Combine 2 tablespoons each pecans, coconut and brown sugar. Heap a generous amount of this mixture atop each potato. Drizzle a tablespoon of melted butter over each, moistening the tops and the sides.

Place the stuffed sweets on a tray and bake for 15 to 20 minutes, or until hot.

Makes 4 servings.

Candied Yams, Apples & Raisins

How sweet they are.

1 cup packed brown sugar
3/4 cup honey
1/2 cup butter
1/4 teaspoon salt
About 4 lbs. yams, cooked until just-tender but not mushy
2 medium-size red apples, unpeeled, cored and cut into 8 slices
1 tablespoon lemon juice
1/2 cup dark or golden raisins
Cinnamon
1/4 cup walnut pieces

◎ In a large heavy skillet, stir together brown sugar, honey, butter and salt and bring to a gentle boil, stirring until butter is melted and mixture is syrupy.

◎ Slice yams into thick circles (or halve lengthwise, if you prefer) and lay them in the simmering syrup. Baste them once, then cover and simmer for 5 minutes over the lowest possible heat. Uncover skillet, turn the yams over gently, and baste again.

◎ Meanwhile, toss apple slices with lemon juice and lay them in the skillet over and around the yams. Sprinkle on the raisins, then top with a light dusting of cinnamon. Baste thoroughly with the hot syrup.

◎ Cover skillet and continue to cook over low heat 10 minutes, basting occasionally. Uncover and cook for an additional 15 minutes or so, spooning syrup over the mixture from time to time. Apples should be tender, yams well glazed, and syrup thickened.

◎ To serve: with a large spoon, remove yams to a platter. Place apple rings on top. Sprinkle on the walnuts and spoon on any syrup left in skillet.

Makes 6 to 8 servings.

Cinnamon Sweet Potato Donuts

A nice surprise for after school snacking.

2 cups whole wheat flour
2 cups unbleached white flour
2 tablespoons baking powder
1 teaspoon salt
1 teaspoon cinnamon
½ teaspoon nutmeg
¼ teaspoon cloves

Oil for deep fat frying
½ cup granulated sugar
1 teaspoon cinnamon

3 eggs
1 cup packed brown sugar
1½ cups mashed cooked sweet
     potatoes
2 tablespoons melted butter
¾ cup half-and-half
1 teaspoon grated orange rind
¾ cup dried currants

- In a medium-size bowl, stir together flours, baking powder, salt, 1 teaspoon cinnamon, nutmeg and cloves; set aside.

- In a large bowl, beat eggs until thick. Beat in the brown sugar, whisking until smooth and creamy. Beat in potatoes and butter until combined. Blend in half-and-half, orange rind and currants.

- Slowly add dry ingredients to sweet potato mixture, stirring until evenly combined. Cover and chill dough at least 4 hours to firm up.

- Roll the chilled dough on a floured board to a thickness of about ½ inch. Cut with a donut cutter and re-roll trimmings until you've used up all your dough. (Do this in 2 batches.) Fry donuts in a pool of deep hot oil (365°) 1 to 1½ minutes per side, turning once, or until well browned and nicely puffed up (as a donut should be). Keep the temperature of the oil constant.

- Stir together ½ cup granulated sugar with 1 teaspoon cinnamon. Remove donuts with a slotted spoon and drain briefly on paper toweling. Roll them in cinnamon-sugar mixture while still hot, until well coated. Serve 'em hot, warm, or cool—any time of day or night.

Makes 36 to 40 donuts.

Cinnamon
Sweet Potato Bread Pudding

4 cups packed dry whole wheat bread cubes (you can use French
  bread, egg bread, or raisin bread also)
1½ cups milk
½ cup half-and-half
4 eggs
1 cup mashed cooked sweet potatoes
½ cup packed brown sugar (light or dark)
1 teaspoon each vanilla and cinnamon
¼ teaspoon cloves
Pinch freshly grated orange rind
½ cup each chopped toasted almonds and golden raisins
¼ cup chopped toasted almonds
Extra cinnamon
1 tablespoon melted butter

🍞 Preheat oven to 350°. Butter a 2-quart casserole dish. Place
the bread cubes in the prepared dish; set aside for now.

🍞 In a blender (or with a wire whisk), blend milk with half-and-
half, eggs, potatoes, sugar, vanilla, 1 teaspoon cinnamon,
cloves and orange rind until well combined.

🍞 Stir the ½ cup almonds and raisins into the bread cubes, dis-
tributing them evenly. Pour the blended custard mixture
over all. Sprinkle with an additional ¼ cup almonds and
some extra cinnamon. Drizzle on the melted butter.

🍞 Place the filled casserole gently into a larger pan containing
an inch of hot water. Bake for 55 to 65 minutes, or until
firm and delicious. (A knife inserted should come out clean.)

🍞 This dish is especially comforting served warm, with heavy
or whipped cream, or French vanilla ice cream.

Makes 6 to 8 servings.

Sweet Potato Biscuits

Surprise your family with these.

1 cup unbleached white flour
¼ cup whole wheat flour
1 tablespoon baking powder
1 tablespoon packed brown sugar
½ teaspoon salt
A few dashes cinnamon and nutmeg
⅓ cup firm butter

1 egg, beaten
½ cup mashed cooked sweet potatoes
2 tablespoons sour cream
~Melted butter~
~Poppyseeds and/or lightly toasted sesame seeds~

Preheat oven to 425°. In a mixing bowl, stir together flours, baking powder, sugar, salt and spices. Cut in ⅓ cup firm butter until mixture resembles cornmeal. (In other words, do as you would when you make pastry—if you make pastry, that is.)

In a small bowl, mix beaten egg with potatoes and sour cream until smooth and evenly combined. Add to the bowl of flour mixture and stir with a fork just until dough holds together.

Briefly knead on a floured board (about 10~12 strokes), then roll or pat dough to a ½~inch thickness. Cut with a biscuit cutter, reusing scraps until you have used up all the dough. Place biscuits on an ungreased baking sheet.

Brush tops lightly with melted butter and sprinkle with poppy or sesame seeds (use some of each for variety). Bake 10 to 12 minutes, or until lightly golden. Serve hot, with Honey~Butter,* if desired.

Makes 8 2½~inch biscuits, or 16 1½~inch biscuits.

*To make Honey~Butter, whip 1 part honey into 3 parts softened butter. Pile into a crock and serve with biscuits, muffins, hotcakes, or even on plain cooked yams or sweet potatoes.

Sweet Potato Hotcakes

1 cup unbleached white flour
1 cup whole wheat flour
1 tablespoon baking powder
½ teaspoon cinnamon
¼ teaspoon ginger
⅛ teaspoon nutmeg
Pinch cloves
¼ teaspoon salt

3 eggs
1½ cups milk
½ cup melted butter
¼ cup honey
½ cup mashed cooked sweet potatoes
½ cup chopped walnuts or sunflower seeds

In a large mixing bowl, stir together flours, baking powder, spices and salt until evenly mixed; set aside.

In a medium~size bowl, whisk eggs until thick. Whisk in the milk, then butter, honey and potatoes. Beat until smooth. Add the nuts or seeds. Fold the wet ingredients into the dry, whisking until thoroughly combined.

Bake on a hot, lightly buttered griddle or skillet, over medium~low heat, until surface bubbles pop, and tops are fairly dry. Brown other sides — turning only once.

Serve right away, with lots of whipped butter and pure maple syrup. Especially nice when accompanied by hot chunky cinnamon applesauce.

Makes 16 medium~size hotcakes.

Golden Sweet Potato & Walnut Bread

Soft and moist ~ cut with a serrated knife.

½ cup butter, softened
2 tablespoons molasses <u>plus</u> honey to equal ¾ cup
2 eggs
1 cup mashed cooked sweet potatoes
¼ cup half~and~half

2 cups whole wheat pastry flour (or half white/half whole wheat)
1 teaspoon cinnamon
½ teaspoon <u>each</u> salt, baking soda and ginger
¼ teaspoon <u>each</u> cloves and allspice
½ cup <u>each</u> chopped walnuts and golden raisins

~Extra chopped walnuts~

- Preheat oven to 350°. Butter a 9~inch loaf pan.

- In a large bowl, beat butter with molasses/honey mixture, eggs and sweet potatoes until blended. Beat in the half~and~half.

- In a separate bowl, stir flour with cinnamon, salt, soda, ginger, cloves and allspice. Add this dry mix to the wet ingre~dients, stirring with a wooden spoon to moisten everything thoroughly. Fold in the ½ cup walnuts and raisins.

- Pour batter into pan. Smooth top and press on some extra chopped walnuts. Bake for 30 minutes, then reduce oven temperature to 325° and bake an additional 40 to 50 min~utes, or until a toothpick inserted in center comes out clean. Cool 10 to 15 minutes before removing to a wire rack to cool completely. Nice served with whipped cream cheese or butter and hot tea.

Makes 1 loaf.

Corn Yam Muffins with Blueberries

1½ cups unbleached flour
½ cup cornmeal
1 tablespoon baking powder
1 teaspoon salt
½ teaspoon <u>each</u> cinnamon and nutmeg
¼ teaspoon <u>each</u> allspice, cloves and ginger

1 egg, beaten
½ cup mashed cooked yams
½ cup milk
¼ cup honey
¼ cup melted butter
¾ cup fresh or frozen blueberries

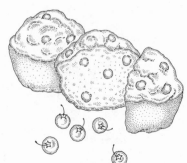

⦿ Preheat oven to 400°. Butter 12 muffin tins.

⦿ In a mixing bowl, stir together flour, cornmeal, baking powder, salt and spices. Make a "well" in the center.

⦿ In a small bowl, whisk together egg, yams, milk, honey and butter until smooth. Add this all at once to the "well" of dry ingredients, mixing with a light hand just until moistened. Gently fold in the blueberries, taking care not to smash them.

⦿ Spoon batter into your prepared tins, filling about ¾ full. Bake about 20 minutes, or until tops turn golden and firm. Serve 'em hot, accompanied by lots of whipped butter and honey.

Makes 12 muffins.

Spiced Sweet Potato & Granola Pudding

⅔ cup packed brown sugar
2½ tablespoons cornstarch
¼ teaspoon salt
½ teaspoon cinnamon
¼ teaspoon ginger
⅛ teaspoon cloves

Toasted Granola Crunch:

½ cup granola (your favorite kind)
2 tablespoons lightly toasted coconut
1 tablespoon melted butter

2 cups milk
½ cup cooked sweet potatoes, puréed or very well mashed
2 egg yolks, beaten
2 tablespoons butter
1 teaspoon vanilla

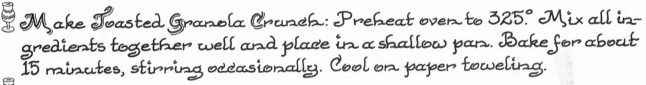

🍷 Make Toasted Granola Crunch: Preheat oven to 325°. Mix all ingredients together well and place in a shallow pan. Bake for about 15 minutes, stirring occasionally. Cool on paper toweling.

🍷 In a medium-size saucepan, stir together sugar, cornstarch, salt and spices. Blend in milk and sweet potatoes. Cook over medium-low heat, whisking constantly until pudding thickens and boils. Boil and stir 2 minutes longer, then remove from heat.

🍷 Stir some of the hot pudding mixture into the beaten yolks, then return this to the saucepan mixture, whisking them together well. Stir over low heat for about 2 more minutes, until pudding is quite thick and creamy.

🍷 Remove from heat and blend in butter and vanilla. Cool slightly, stirring from time to time.

🍷 Into clear parfait or pudding cups, layer warm pudding with Toasted Granola Crunch. Chill, or serve slightly warm.

Makes 4 servings.

Maple Sweet Potato Pie
with Buttery Pastry Crust

You may like this better than pumpkin.

The Filling:
3 eggs
2 cups mashed cooked sweet
   potatoes
2/3 cup packed light~brown
   sugar
1/3 cup granulated sugar
1 teaspoon cinnamon
1/2 teaspoon each ginger and salt
1/4 teaspoon nutmeg
1/8 teaspoon cloves
1/4 teaspoon maple extract
1¼ cups half~and~half

~Whipped cream, lightly sweetened~
~Pure maple syrup or nutmeg~

The Crust:
3/4 cup unbleached white
   flour
1/4 cup whole wheat flour
1/4 teaspoon salt
1/3 cup cold butter
3 tablespoons cold milk

🥧 Prepare Buttery Pastry Crust: In a mixing bowl, thoroughly stir together flours and salt. Cut in butter with a pastry blender until mixture resembles coarse meal.

🥧 Drizzle in the milk stirring lightly with a fork to incorporate it evenly. Form into a ball, then flatten into a circle.

🥧 Roll out on a cloth~covered board until approximately 1/8 inch thick, rolling from the center as you go. Fit the pastry into a 9~inch pie plate (do not stretch), then crimp the edges decoratively. Refrigerate pastry if not using immediately.

🥧 Preheat oven to 350.°

🥧 Make filling: In a large bowl, beat eggs until blended. Beat in potatoes, sugars, cinnamon, ginger, salt, nutmeg, cloves and maple extract until uniform. Add the half~and~half, beating until mixture is smooth and creamy. Pour into your awaiting pie shell.

🥧 Bake about 55 to 60 minutes, or until the point of a sharp knife inserted in the center comes out clean. Cool on a wire rack.

🥧 To garnish, decorate edge and center of pie with whipped cream, then drizzle the cream with maple syrup or a light dusting of nutmeg. May be eaten warm or cold.

Makes 1 9~inch pie.

Yam Streusel Coffee Cake

½ cup butter, softened
1½ cups sugar
3 eggs
1 teaspoon vanilla
¼ teaspoon maple extract
1 cup mashed cooked yams
¼ cup sour cream
2 tablespoons fresh orange juice
½ teaspoon grated orange rind

2 cups flour
1 teaspoon each baking powder
  and baking soda
1 teaspoon cinnamon
¼ teaspoon salt
1 cup golden raisins

Streusel Mixture:

½ cup packed dark brown sugar
2 tablespoons butter, softened
2 tablespoons flour
1 teaspoon cinnamon
½ cup diced walnuts

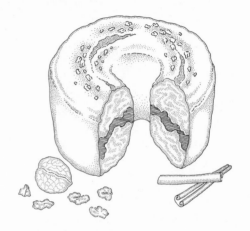

Preheat oven to 350°. Butter a tube or bundt pan. In a large bowl, cream together butter and sugar. Beat in eggs, one at a time until fluffy. Beat in vanilla, maple extract, yams, sour cream, orange juice and rind until creamy and smooth.

In a separate bowl, stir together flour, baking powder, baking soda, cinnamon and salt until combined. Gradually blend this into the creamed mixture until uniform. Stir in the raisins.

Combine all streusel ingredients in a small bowl. Into your pre~pared pan, spoon in ½ of the batter, smoothing top to make an even layer. Sprinkle on ½ of the streusel mixture. Repeat this procedure, ending with a final layer of streusel.

Bake cake for 1 hour to 1 hour and 15 minutes, or until a tooth~pick inserted into the cake comes out clean. Cool for about 30 minutes before removing from pan. Serve at room temper~ature or slightly warm.

Makes 1 large coffee cake.

Other

CREATIVE

POTATO IDEAS

Mastering
The Fine Art of Garnishing

Serving a stuffed potato skin without a garnish is almost like serving a hot fudge sundae without a maraschino cherry! It just isn't complete. Garnishing food is the final step in any recipe — be it a dusting of paprika or a generous heap of sour cream.

The proper garnish makes your finished potato dish even more tempting and pleasing to the eye — a real work of art, you might say. Experienced chefs know that a properly prepared meal is something which looks as wonderful as it tastes. Garnishes for stuffed potato skins can be as simple or as sophisticated as you like, but please keep in mind a few do's and don'ts.

DO'S AND DON'TS:

~ <u>Don't</u> overpower the filling with a heavy garnish that doesn't relate well. The filling and garnish should harmonize.

~ <u>Do</u> use color contrast, like a mild quiche filling sprinkled with chopped scallions or chili and beans garnished with sour cream. It should be eye-catching!

~ <u>Do</u> be aware of contrasting flavors and textures as well. For example: steamed veggies topped with a spicy sauce or crunchy almonds sprinkled over a creamy seafood filling

~ <u>Don't</u> be afraid to experiment with whatever you happen to have around. The garnishes in these recipes can be altered to suit your own taste buds. Feel free to use more than one garnish, too.

A SIMPLE LIST OF SIMPLE GARNISHES:

1. Grated cheese. Try your favorites, but please experiment with the unfamiliar as well.
2. Chopped onions ~ white, green or red ~ chives, too.
3. Olives ~ whole (pitted), sliced or chopped. There are green, black, pimento ~ stuffed, marinated, etc...
4. Sour cream, plain yogurt, mayonnaise ~ these all add smoothness.
5. Fresh herbs ~ parsley, cilantro, dill, basil, etc. Chop or use fresh sprigs.
6. Nuts and seeds ~ almonds, cashews, peanuts; sesame and sunflower seeds, etc. Delicious both raw and toasted.
7. Chopped tomatoes or whole cherry tomatoes.
8. Bacon ~ cooked and crumbled. Or use soy bacon bits.
9. Pimentos ~ strips or diced.
10. Green chilies ~ ditto.
11. Fruits ~ for sweetness. Try raisins, pineapple chunks, coconut (white or toasted), an orange or lemon twist...
12. Chutney ~ just a dab, for added elegance.
13. Sprouts ~ bean, alfalfa, lentil... for a healthier potato skin.
14. Dried herbs and seasonings ~ paprika, chili powder, dillweed, fresh ground pepper, etc.
15. Quick sauces ~ pizza, tarter, cheese...
16. Chopped raw vegetables ~ try one or mix them together. Some favorites: radishes, mushrooms, carrots, zucchini, celery, cucumber, sweet green peas. May be marinated or mixed with a light dressing.
17. Crisp salad greens or cabbage ~ finely shredded or chopped for a refreshing crunch.
18. Chinese fried noodles ~ good on lots of potato skin dishes.
19. Hard cooked eggs ~ chopped or sliced.
20. Buttered bread crumbs.
21. Toasted wheat germ mixed with melted butter and Parmesan.
22. Salsa ~ mild to spicy.
23. Guacamole ~ chunky and good!
24. Red and green bell peppers ~ finely diced.
25. Crispy fried tortilla strips or corn chips.

Last Minute Potato Toppers

So, you're definitely in a potato mood! Nothing sounds better than a whole baked potato or some crispy skins, overflowing with something hot and savory, or cool and soothing. Here you'll find some simple, last minute suggestions to help satisfy that potato craving at a moment's notice. As long as you have a nice-sized baked potato handy, or some skins waiting to be filled, there is a wonderful potato entrée ahead of you.

Topping a Whole Baked Potato — in a Flash

I almost always have extra baked potatoes hanging around. They're just incomparable for on-the-spot meals. Sometimes I use them in a quick potato salad, or I chop and sauté them with scrambled eggs or omelette fillings. But really, the <u>best</u> way to use a once hot baked potato is to reheat it (in a microwave or conventional oven), then top it with one of the many suggestions that follow.

<u>Note</u>: Before serving, reheat your potato(es) until steamy-hot while preparing the topping ingredients. Cut through the surface in the usual fashion, then squeeze it open before ladeling on your topping.

Potato Skin Fillings — in a Hurry

The trick to whipping out a potato skin dinner (or breakfast, brunch or lunch) is having ready-made potato skins available in your refrigerator. Read the section entitled "Make Ahead Skins" so you'll always be prepared. Assuming you have the skins on hand, and they're crisped or fried, all that's left to do is conjure up a favorite filling.

There are some minor differences to filling up a potato skin as opposed to topping a whole baked potato. Keep these pointers in mind as you read through the following list of potato toppings and fillings.

~ When serving skins, you do not eat the potato innards, so you are likely to consume more unless the filling is very heavy or the skins are extra large. Plan on about two filled skins per person.

~ Serve one whole topped baked potato per person. The larger the potato, the better.

~ With skins, there should be less sauce and more substance to the filling to constitute a substantial meal.

~ The skin is just a "shell" (like a piecrust) to support the filling, which is really the main attraction.

~ Whole baked potatoes love saucy toppings which can be stirred through the potatoes as they are being eaten, making it a fun as well as a delicious experience.

~ Not Just Sour Cream and Chives Anymore ~

SOME DELECTABLE LAST MINUTE POTATO TOPPINGS & FILLINGS

1. Grated cheese with crumbled real bacon or soy bacon bits. A sharp cheddar is nice, but try Swiss, Jack, Brie, fresh grated Parmesan, etc. Broil until nicely melted.

2. Whip together softened cream cheese, chopped black olives and sliced scallions; mound on potatoes and heat gently.

3. Sautéed mushrooms with the addition of sour cream and just a hint of dry sherry.

4. Cut up hard-cooked eggs mixed into a cream sauce seasoned with dill or curry.

5. Cooked chicken, cut into thin strips, moistened with a mild chili salsa, topped with cheddar and heated...yum!

6. A mound of cottage cheese, chives, seasoned salt and pepper.

7. Hot dogs cut diagonally into thin slices, heated with catsup or barbecue sauce. Spoon on sweet pickle rel~

ish and chopped onion.

8. Hot creamed corn. Extra good with the addition of crumbled bacon and/or cheese.

9. Sautéed chicken livers with diced bacon, thinly sliced onion and a dash of dry sherry. Stir in some sour cream or plain yogurt before topping your spud or skins.

10. Chopped fresh tomato, avocado, onion and green chilies (canned). Season with salt and pepper. How about a dab of mayonnaise?

mix &
match
11. Guacamole, sour cream and salsa.

12. Hot refried beans and melted Jack or cheddar cheese.

13. A hot, thick cream soup such as asparagus, tomato, split pea with ham, navy bean or chowders like clam, corn and cheese. Many possibilities here.

14. Flaked smoked fish, with sour cream and butter.

15. Hot chili con carne, garnished with shredded cheese and fresh chopped onion. Top with corn chips.

16. Sautéed breakfast sausages with scrambled eggs. Cheese enthusiasts… melt on something mild, like Jack or Muenster.

17. Any creamed vegetable will do just fine. Try tiny pearl onions or peas.

18. Stir-fried veggies and soy sauce. Top with toasted nuts for a pleasant crunch.

19. Tofu chunks, soy sauce and a few drops of Chinese sesame oil.

20. Chunks of bleu cheese, sliced black olives and minced scallions mixed into sour cream with a dash of dill.

21. Pizza sauce from a jar topped with lots of mozzarella and Parmesan, then broiled until gooey. Tuck in some Italian salami if you happen to have it around.

22. Canned or homemade salsa or enchilada sauce, heated and topped with lots of cheddar or Jack. Broil.

23. Baked beans with the optional addition of diced ham, cooked bacon or ground beef, or thin slices of hot dog. Sprinkle with diced sweet onion.

24. Canned salmon or tuna in a cream sauce with hard-cooked eggs and dill weed.

25. Lots of onions sautéed with red and green bell pepper strips and chunks of smoked ham. Can be topped with cheese and broiled.

26. Nuts (cashews, almonds, peanuts) stir-fried in butter, sprinkled generously over creamy melted cheese.

27. How about diced salami or pepperoni with sliced olives and broiled Provolone?

28. A heap of ricotta mixed with Italian herbs and topped with grated fresh Romano cheese. Bake or broil.

29. Crabmeat or shrimp blended with sautéed scallions, a hint of garlic and thinly sliced mushrooms. To finish, melt on some grated Jack or Swiss cheese.

30. Shredded ham or corned beef strips and Swiss with a dab of Dijon mustard. Heat to melt the cheese.

31. Quick "Pesto Potatoes" — Your hot potato (or skins) smothered in a robust sauce of olive oil, fresh basil, garlic and Parmesan. Top with pine nuts for an exotic crunch.

32. Quick "Alfredo Potato" — Make an extra rich white sauce with the addition of Parmesan cheese. Blend in some freshly steamed broccoli, cauliflower or spinach.

LEFTOVER POTATO TOPPERS & FILLERS

Leftovers are not as bad as we're led to believe. In fact, with a little ingenuity, they can be the start of a whole new dining experience. All you need is a piping hot baked potato or some crispy skins followed by a spark of your own imagination. The result...a delicious, quick and economical main course. What follows are some suggestions you can use to make those leftovers better the second time around. A final bit of advice—serve 'em up HOT!

1. Thick stews, soups or stroganoff, gently reheated.

2. Sauces or gravies like cheese, creamy chicken, mornay, curry, etc. Thin with a bit of milk or cream, add pieces of leftover meat and/or vegetables and warm over low heat.
   Other Ideas: ~Giblet gravy with extra chopped turkey and the last of the vegetables.
   ~Spaghetti sauce with Italian sausage, chopped up hamburger patties, the last of the meat loaf, or meatballs. Don't forget the Parmesan!

3. Cooked flaked fish, reheated in melted lemon~butter with your favorite herb. Top with sour cream.

4. The last of a soufflé or quiche. Watch closely as you reheat.

5. Roast beef strips in gravy or au jus—heated and accompanied by a spoonful of sour cream or plain yogurt mixed with horseradish

6. Barbecued beef or pork served hot. Pass chopped fresh onion to sprinkle on top.

QUICK & DELICIOUS BUTTER, SOUR CREAM & CREAM CHEESE TOPPERS

I know it's hard to break out of the old butter, sour cream and chives pattern of topping your baked potatoes. I've been there myself. To educate you slowly, I have combined your favorite potato toppings with a few staples you are most likely to have on hand right now. The result is something extraordinary and guaranteed delicious. Each recipe will adorn 4 to 6 large, whole baked potatoes.

Soft Butter Toppers: Let ½ cup butter (1 stick) come to room temperature. With a wooden spoon, cream butter together with one or more of your favorite herbs. Try parsley, thyme, basil, oregano, dill, etc. Use 1 tablespoon fresh or ½ teaspoon dried herbs (more, to taste). Blend in grated sharp cheese if you wish. How about adding 2 tablespoons of lightly toasted sesame or sunflower seeds?

Sour Cream Toppers: Start with 1 cup of real sour cream. For something Oniony, stir in 2 or more tablespoons of minced chives or scallions, 1 teaspoon of seasoned salt and a dash of garlic powder. For something Cheesy, blend in ¼ cup grated Parmesan, Romano or Swiss. Crumble in some cooked bacon or soy bacon bits. For something Mexican, slowly add mild or hot salsa to your sour cream, stopping just when you've achieved the right zest. Mix in some sliced black olives, if you dare. For something Curried, stir in approximately 1 teaspoon of curry powder along with ½ teaspoon of salt and a dash of cayenne. Top with toasted sliced almonds or chopped cashews. Note: Plain lowfat yogurt can be substituted for all or part of the sour cream to cut down on fat. Choose a firm yogurt. Or, whip up a batch of Buttermilk Sour Cream (see recipe page 156).

Cream Cheese Toppers: Beat 1 8-oz. package cream cheese, softened, with 4 to 6 tablespoons half-and-half or milk until fluffy and smooth. For something Nutty, stir in ¼ cup chopped toasted almonds, cashews or peanuts. Salt to taste. For something Smoky, blend in 4 slices of crumbled cooked bacon and 1 large minced scallion. Another good thing to crumble in — Roquefort or bleu cheese. Note: A cup of regular or lowfat cottage cheese can be substituted for the cream cheese. Press it through a sieve first, then beat in one or two of the accouterments, omitting the half-and-half or milk.

The Potato Party

Please don't confuse a Potato Party with any sort of political party, or even the infamous pajama party. Instead, guests come on this occasion tastefully dressed and eagerly prepared to sample an abundant (not to mention delightful) assortment of potato skin recipes.

You can offer Seafood Skins, Appetizer Skins, Chicken Skins, etc., plus a variety of dips surrounded by crispy Skin Chips. How about setting up a "Potato Bar?" It's somewhat like a salad bar, only you serve steaming hot baked potatoes on large plates or bowls, and for condiments you present a selection of potato toppings and garnishes fit for royalty. See the section "Last Minute Potato Toppers" for an astonishing array of ideas. This way, your ecstatic guests can spoon on condiments to their hearts' desire. Still another method is to set up a hot buffet of different fillings, toppings and garnishes, and serve them with a large basketful of warm crisped or fried skins so each participant can make his or her own Potato Skin Creation.

Here are some helpful tips to guide you on your merry way:

1~ Accentuate variety. Offer skins with a wide range of fillings, toppings and garnishes. Vary textures too—smooth, crispy, chunky, crunchy. Make some mild, make some spicy.

2~ Try planning your Potato Party around a foreign country. Serve ethnic~style skins or set up a "Potato Bar" with toppings expressing the foods of that land. For instance, Italian potatoes crave spicy sausages, creamy ricotta, robust herbs and freshly grated Parmesan. Mexican potatoes adore fiery sauces, chunky guacamole, cool sour cream and zesty meats. Have your guests dress authentically for a special atmospheric touch.

3~ To keep the filled skins hot (or the fillings, in case of a do~it~yourself approach), chafing dishes come in handy. Some electric skillets can work also, as do certain styles of crock pots.

4~ If you're timid about giving parties, relax. A Potato Party is an excellent way for people to meet, enjoy good food, and partake in friendly conversation all at the same time. Watch spirits soar as your guests sample your skins and invent their own edible potato concoctions. No one is left out of the fun.

5~ How about a contest for the best potato creation and/or who can eat the most potato skins? For the prize...a 10~pound sack of russets!

Index

Photograph by Paul Tanner

*L*isa Wolfson Tanner was born in 1957 in Los Angeles, California. She graduated with a Bachelor of Fine Arts from California State University, Long Beach, where she made food illustration her forte.

Besides being quite busy writing and illustrating two books in the past two-and-a-half years (her first, *The Brownie Experience*, Ten Speed Press, 1984), Lisa enjoys oil painting, teaching art classes, jogging, and being with her three-year-old daughter, Jessica, whom she adores.

Lisa says there are more books and projects in her future, and that this is only the beginning of a very rewarding and fulfilling way of self-expression.